T0328796

Cambridge Elements ☰

Elements in Language, Gender and Sexuality
edited by
Helen Sauntson
York St John University
Holly R. Cashman
University of New Hampshire

THE LANGUAGE OF GENDER-BASED SEPARATISM

A Comparative Analysis

Veronika Koller
Lancaster University

Alexandra Krendel
Lancaster University

Jessica Aiston
Lancaster University

CAMBRIDGE
UNIVERSITY PRESS

Shaftesbury Road, Cambridge CB2 8EA, United Kingdom

One Liberty Plaza, 20th Floor, New York, NY 10006, USA

477 Williamstown Road, Port Melbourne, VIC 3207, Australia

314–321, 3rd Floor, Plot 3, Splendor Forum, Jasola District Centre,
New Delhi – 110025, India

103 Penang Road, #05–06/07, Visioncrest Commercial, Singapore 238467

Cambridge University Press is part of Cambridge University Press & Assessment,
a department of the University of Cambridge.

We share the University's mission to contribute to society through the pursuit of
education, learning and research at the highest international levels of excellence.

www.cambridge.org
Information on this title: www.cambridge.org/9781009216869

DOI: 10.1017/9781009216890

First published 2023

A catalogue record for this publication is available from the British Library.

ISBN 978-1-009-21686-9 Paperback
ISSN 2634-8772 (online)
ISSN 2634-8764 (print)

The Language of Gender-Based Separatism

A Comparative Analysis

Elements in Language, Gender and Sexuality

DOI: 10.1017/9781009216890
First published online: July 2023

Veronika Koller
Lancaster University

Alexandra Krendel
Lancaster University

Jessica Aiston
Lancaster University

Author for correspondence: Veronika Koller, v.koller@lancaster.ac.uk

Abstract: This Element shows how two social movements and networks, lesbian separatism and Men Going Their Own Way (MGTOW), reflect the changing and complex (anti-)feminist ideologies of their time. The authors outline the historical and political background of those discourses and how they are influencing contemporary gender relations.

The materials analysed comprise ten manifestos, which are examined with a combination of data-led discourse analysis and theory-led argumentation analysis. The manifestos are similar in that both sets of authors construct homogenous in-groups and out-groups as well as dichotomies between them. There are some differences though in how this is linguistically realised and who is classified as an out-group. Both groups cast social actors in particular roles and establish ethical norms, but strategic planning and utopias are more prominent among lesbian separatists. Freedom, advantage and authority are central in each group's argumentation, but lesbian separatists also stress humanitarianism while MGTOW focus on financial matters.

Keywords: feminism, manosphere, manifestos, social movements, lesbian discourse

ISBNs: 9781009216869 (PB), 9781009216890 (OC)
ISSNs: 2634-8772 (online), 2634-8764 (print)

Contents

1 Introduction

In this Element, we examine the manifestos of a gender-based separatism movement and network, respectively. We analyse texts by lesbian separatists and Men Going Their Own Way (hereafter referred to as MGTOW) in order to establish the similarities and differences between them. Lesbian separatism is a mostly historical movement in which women distanced themselves from both men and from women who pursued relationships with men. In some cases, this involved purchasing land and developing residential collectives; alternatively, lesbians formed collectively run businesses. MGTOW is a part of the broad online anti-feminist network known as the manosphere, in which mostly heterosexual men advocate abstaining from relationships with women to varying degrees (e.g., avoiding marriage or sexual relationships). Comparing the discourses of these two gender-based separatist groups shows how they influence contemporary gender relations; more specifically, the study helps throw light on how language use can sustain the toxic masculinity of the manosphere. Moreover, our research also traces the roots of the current debate around (trans) women's rights.

Gender-based separatism must be analytically distinguished from gender segregation (or 'sex segregation', as most authors call it). Cohen (2011) defines such segregation as 'laws, rules, or policies that require complete separation of men and women or that completely exclude either men or women from participating in an activity' (pp. 57–8). Conversely, Frye (1978) explains that female separatism comprises separation 'from men and from institutions, relationships, roles, and activities which are male-defined, male-dominated and operating for the benefit of males' and is crucially 'initiated or maintained, at will, *by women*' (p. 31, original emphasis). Thus, while segregation is imposed in a top-down manner by way of laws and policies, separatism is practised from below. For example, segregation includes male- or female-only schools, prisons, military units, workplaces and public toilets (Reskin, 1993; Cohen, 2011), whereas separatism encompasses practices such as avoiding heterosexual relationships, refusing to consume sexist media or forbidding people of the perceived 'opposite' sex to enter one's home (Frye, 1978). Separatism is usually a liberationist movement in which people who are disempowered on the grounds of, for example, gender, ethnicity, religion or nationality seek to gain power by withdrawing from dominant groups in their respective societies. It is therefore no surprise that we find few examples of male separatism. Indeed, MGTOW's aim to have no or only limited relations with women is based on their belief that men are oppressed in contemporary Western society.

Separatism is perhaps better known in the context of national and regional conflicts, such as the tensions about the Tamil secessionist movement (Sri Lanka), the wish for independence in Catalonia (Spain) and Scotland (United Kingdom) or the historical conflict over the Republic of Biafra (Nigeria). Understood as an expression of regional or national identity, separatism 'aims to reduce the political and other powers of the central government of a state over a particular territory and to transfer those powers to the population ... of the territory in question' (Pavković & Cabestan, 2013, p. 1). The conflicts that both trigger and are caused by national and regional separatism mean that the word 'separatism' can itself become a contested signifier: while it is often imbued with negative connotations by political majorities, such evaluations are questioned and subverted by those wishing to form a new state by breaking away from a larger state (Karpenko-Seccombe, 2021). It is the positive view of separatism that Jill Johnston drew on in her book *Lesbian Nation*, in which she metaphorically extended the idea of national to gender-based separatism (see Koller, 2010), declaring that 'an oppressed group must withdraw into itself to establish its own identity and rebuild its strength through mutual support and recognition' (1973, pp. 166–7). Despite Johnston's claim that 'unless all women are lesbians, there will be no true political revolution' (1973, p. 166), however, not all gender-based separatism revolves around homosexuality. The mostly heterosexual MGTOW's search for sovereignty is a case in point, as are instances of workplace separatism. As a term introduced by Brewer (1995), workplace separatism refers to usually women withdrawing from mixed organisational settings and instead forming their own, single-sex businesses or organisations. Examples range from networks for female entrepreneurs to women's collectives in developing countries (e.g., Kamra & Sen, 2021).

Comparing the two forms of gender-based separatism that we investigate in this Element, MGTOW has been described by one commentator on the manosphere as 'a lot like lesbian separatism, but for straight dudes' (Futrelle, n.d.), which anticipates similarities but also differences between the two separatist communities. It is notable that members of both communities share(d) their experiences with other members and encourage(d) each others' beliefs to develop. For lesbian separatists, this practice took the form of feminist consciousness-raising groups, whereas for MGTOW, the process of realising perceived truths about society and gender relations is called 'taking the red pill'. However, it is important to acknowledge that the two communities reflect different phenomena. Lesbian separatism was tied to, although not identical with, radical feminism of the 1970s and 1980s, which sought to end power imbalances between men and women, whereas MGTOW is part of a wider backlash against the gains that women have made as a result of feminism. Thus, we do not seek to claim that the two movements are equivalent in their stance or in their degree of radicalism. Rather, our aim in this Element is to investigate in an empirical manner whether Futrelle's assertion that the two share similarities is true. We do this by examining the language used in manifestos by both lesbian separatists and MGTOW.

Having introduced the topic of gender-based separatism, the rest of the Element is structured as follows. In Section 2, we describe lesbian separatists and MGTOW in more detail, paying particular attention to their historical backgrounds. In Section 3, we discuss the extent to which lesbian separatism and MGTOW can be classified as social movements, and we introduce literature on what constitutes a manifesto. Following this, Section 4 introduces the manifestos that make up our data set and explains the methods we use to investigate these manifestos, namely inductive, data-led qualitative discourse analysis and deductive, theory-led argumentation analysis. In Sections 5 and 6, we showcase our findings from the lesbian separatist and MGTOW texts, respectively, and in Section 7, we note the similarities and differences between the manifestos and consider the extent to which these discourses can be considered extremist. We then conclude in Section 8 by summarising the contributions of our study and by noting interesting directions for future research on both lesbian separatists and MGTOW.

2 Forms of Gender-Based Separatism

In this section, we provide some background to lesbian separatism and MGTOW as a gender-based separatist movement and network, respectively, in order to contextualise our data and help to later explain the findings from our analysis (Sections 5 and 6).

2.1 Lesbian Separatism

Female separatism is practised to a degree whenever women create spaces which are exclusive to themselves in order to further political or economic causes. In the highly politicised lesbian discourse of the 1970s, separatism was seen by many as the logical extension of feminism. Considering the patriarchal conditions women were subjected to, it seemed logical to the advocates of separatism that all women would have to be lesbians and all lesbians separatists (Lettice, 1987, p. 109). Women who maintained relations of any kind with men were seen by separatists as unable to dissociate themselves from a society structured in sexist and heteronormative terms. The final goal was to overthrow patriarchy and the way by which this goal would be achieved was through a total withdrawal of female energy from men. Based on the notion of 'parasitism of males on females' (Frye, 1978, p. 33), the dominant male system was thought to collapse when it was denied the 'mental, spiritual, and physical' female energy it exploits (MacDonald, 2015). Any form of co-operation with men, even for liberationist politics such as gay rights or anti-racism, therefore runs counter to the idea of separatism. Indeed, many Black feminists took a stance against gender-based separatism and instead opted to work with Black men in the civil rights movement, while also seeking to educate them about feminist issues (see Combahee River Collective, 1977). For lesbian separatists, however, even debating issues of oppression and liberation with out-group members is thought to be counterproductive, because ' [w]hen we engage in a system ... we contribute by consensus to its underlying structure even when also challenging it' (Hoagland, 1987, p. 25).

Retrospective accounts of lesbian separatism have emphasised that the movement was important as a revolutionary vanguard and helped women build a community, but was not intended as 'a realistic, indeterminately future' vision of the world (Johnston, 2006). Others stress that separatism 'is not an ideology, but rather a feminist process, a method for living in the world' and an inspiring utopia (Enszer, 2014, p. 1). According to its advocates, separatism makes it possible for women to develop a community with a 'shared language [and] the opportunity for self-love' (MacDonald, 2015). It is helpful to think of separatism as a continuum, with women realising a greater or lesser degree of living without men. Indeed, many lesbians found their social, sexual and working lives to revolve around women, not necessarily as a conscious choice but as a logical result of their interests and attraction. These women did not necessarily identify as separatists:

> I think that separatism was regarded as something positive by many, many women in the late 1970s. By older as well as by younger women. That was certainly seen as something which enabled women to experience themselves completely independent of everything. . . . Among my friends there were a lot who had very separatist tendencies. (interview with Ina Feder, quoted in Koller, 2008, p. 117)

Like any radical movement, lesbian separatists may not have constituted a large proportion of feminists, perhaps not even lesbian feminists. However, it is important to remember that their uncompromising politics and prolific publishing meant 'pushing the boundaries' for others (Larman, 2019), by making more radical demands and thereby inspiring non-separatists to broaden their agenda.

Although lesbian separatism is based on the idea of withdrawal from, and exclusion of, men, the movement was to go further and create a veritable counter-reality, re-defining such broad concepts as 'ethics, language, sexuality, culture' (Geraldine, 1988, p. 5), along with new forms of spirituality. There were economic aspects, too, as separatists set up businesses, events and networks to distribute publications and music (Gush, 2015). That counter-society was meant to entail a counter-discourse empowering the women who participated in it. To reach that goal, every manifestation of patriarchal discourse – including not only linguistic artefacts but also music, paintings and so on – was to be removed from the life of a lesbian separatist. This seclusion led to self-reliance and the emergence of women's housing and work co-operatives in the 1970s and 1980s. While women in urban areas formed task-oriented collectives (e.g., in publishing), and some separatists collectives lived as travellers on the road (Levy, 2009), residential separatist communities were often geographically located in the countryside, especially in the United States, as contact with men could be more easily avoided there (Shugar, 1995, p. 57; Archibald, 2021). Additionally, 'women's land' seemed to promise a closer relation with nature, which was perceived as the paradigmatic female raped by male power and technology and therefore became an important topic in separatist discourse. This focus on nature as female indicates the links between lesbian separatism and cultural feminism, both of which were prone to essentialism and biological definitions of females (Mackay, 2021, pp. 57–9). However, the hard physical work involved, along with a lack of skills and experience of previously urban separatists, meant that most separatist country communities lasted less than ten years. As one woman remembers it:

> We didn't have country living skills or communal living skills and we didn't have good ways to solve conflicts. . . . I also learned that separatism was a very defensive position. It didn't change the power of women. (Moore, 2020)

Although the women's land movement has been described as 'a once thriving community, now in steady decline' (Savage, 2019), for a certain period of time, land-based, travelling or urban separatism was the ideal for many lesbian feminists.

At their heyday in the 1970s and early 1980s, separatists lived in all-women communities as much as possible to gain complete independence from men. The latter decade, however, saw a number of wide-reaching socio-political changes. In the United States and the UK, the Reagan and Thatcher governments, respectively, ushered in an economic climate that was characterised by lower taxes and less public funding, privatisation and a focus on individual wealth creation through investment. These changes had profound effects on a lesbian community that had, for the better part, not only espoused a collectivist ethos, but also crucially relied on public funding for projects and space. The general paradigm shift away from collectivism and towards individualism that began in the 1980s led to a relative decentring of the lesbian separatist community and had many women redirect their focus (Stein, 1997, p. 131). Under the impression of the individualist ideology of the day, it must have seemed tempting to replace the downwardly mobile life in the lesbian feminist 'subsistence community' (Wolf, 1979, p. 101) with the prospect of a more comfortable existence, even if that ultimately came at the cost of less solidarity. Cox (1993, p. 63) describes such effects of hegemony in a very vivid simile: 'Hegemony is like a pillow: it absorbs blows and sooner or later the would-be assailant will find it comfortable to rest upon.'

On a material level, withdrawing into the private sphere was, in Britain, facilitated by Thatcher's policy of promoting private home ownership and enabling women to buy property in their own name without a male guarantor. As a consequence, in 1980s Britain, local friendship communities evolved around refurbishing newly bought houses. While housing as a social practice is a crucial element in building any community, its significance for lesbian communities changed dramatically, from enabling collective living to an expression of wealth, individualism and coupledom. In addition, the AIDS crisis that started in the 1980s led to renewed collaboration with gay men, and many separatists who were active in the environmentalist and peace movement saw some of their causes evaporate with the changing face of world politics towards the end of the decade. For instance, Healey (1996, p. 78) outlines how the feminist protests at UK cruise missile base Greenham Common, which had begun in 1983, gave rise to separatist camps that dissolved when the missiles were destroyed at the end of the Cold War in 1989.

Other pressures on the separatist movement were internally generated. Oppressive behaviour, explained in Marxist terms as 'false consciousness' by separatist theory, reared its ugly head in the form of racism and class bias (Shugar, 1995, pp. 94–9). Indeed, it was often middle-class women who chose to live as separatists and most of them were white. Their choice of separatism was in part motivated by being disillusioned with both the gay liberation and the wider feminist movement, which they perceived as ignoring lesbians at best and being hostile towards them at worst. Black women, however, also had allegiances with the civil rights and Black Power movements and despite issues of sexism there,

> many . . . feminists of color in the second wave didn't see an intrinsic value in separating from the mixed-gender communities that had raised and empowered them in a world run and dominated by white people in order to throw in their lot with white feminists who didn't prioritize or understand their needs. (Carmen, 2015)

On a theoretical level, Black writers such as bell hooks rejected the idea of sexism as the root cause of all oppression, instead maintaining that oppression stems from Western thinking and its 'belief that the superior should control the inferior' (hooks, 2005, p. 234). That racist discrimination should exist in their community was a cruel realisation for separatists, many of whom 'felt they were free of the behaviours that oppressed them' (Shugar, 1995, p. 95). Splits were also brought about by the exclusion of bisexual and trans women, and by the question whether boy children should be allowed in separatist communities, a debate which hurt and estranged many women (Stein, 1997, p. 119).

In the face of such external pressures and internal tensions, the separatist movement saw itself as cornered and, by many accounts, gradually began to turn its energy and aggression inwards. In some part, such a development was afforded by the very beliefs that form the foundation of separatism. Separatism in its ideal form was meant to be woman-centred, prioritising women's needs and concerns. This woman-centred approach had one major drawback, however, in that it saw the way women lived their lives as the 'subject of revolution' (Star, 1982, p. 67), thus shifting the onus of effecting social change onto women. Later accounts of that inward redirection differ; while some emphasise that 'lesbian separatism was never a prescriptive code for behaviour or relationships [but] a way to figure out what it meant to be a woman' (Gush, 2015), others felt that separatism had 'stopped being a crazy, wonderful experiment' and had become 'a dogma' (Doyle, 1996, p. 185).

It seems safe to claim that as a social movement, lesbian separatism is now defunct. That is not to say, however, that separatist beliefs and ideals have ceased to exist. Indeed, while there is a perception that 'lesbian separatism is a maligned social and cultural formation inside and outside of feminism' (Enszer, 2014, p. 1), it has also enjoyed some re-evaluation, and seminal texts continue to be referenced. For example, the opening of the Radicalesbians' 1970 manifesto *The Woman Identified Woman* – 'A lesbian is the rage of all women condensed to the point of explosion'– is quoted in a podcast half a century later (Unter & Kelly, 2020), where the metaphor is also extended to 'th[e]n I am a black hole' and the transcript comes with the animated image of an erupting volcano.[1]

Some contemporary writers see current women's spaces as 'places where diversity and difference are embraced, not feared', where intersectionality can be acknowledged and where identities can be positively reinforced (Carmen, 2015). Perhaps the most pressing question for separatism today is one that has sparked an often polarised debate in wider society, namely how to define who is

---

[1] For an analysis of the Radicalesbians' manifesto, see Koller (2008, pp. 48–58).

a woman in the first place. Some, especially older, separatists do not accept trans women as women, arguing that trans women pose a threat to women's spaces (Jo et al., 2015) or claiming that 'transactivism erases lesbians' (Get the L out, n.d.). The latter proposition refers to both trans women being seen as threatening women's spaces and trans men being perceived as lesbians who cannot accept their sexuality. In sharp contrast, others believe that separatism can be extended to 'fight the binary altogether', seeing that 'woman and man don't really feel like fixed terms' anymore (Unter & Kelly, 2020). We will return to these divergent positions in Section 8.

Yet perhaps the most significant change is that access to lesbian separatist discourse is no longer restricted to women. Before the advent of the internet, separatist texts were not only produced by women, but were exclusively distributed to, and read by, women as well. As one account states, '[w]e sold only by subscription, or in women's bookstores. Sometimes we sold the magazine in person as we toured the country' (Gush, 2015). These days, separatists and their writings, and discussions on the topic, can be found online, where anyone can access them. This would have been anathema to the core notion of separatism in previous decades but of course helps to build networks now. We will return to the ethical aspects of restricted texts in Section 4; for now, we will move on to provide an overview of the digitally born network of MGTOW.

2.2 Men Going Their Own Way

The men's rights movement has its roots in the men's liberation movement, itself an offshoot of second-wave feminism. During the late 1960s and early 1970s, some men began to engage with feminist activism and so-called 'men's liberation' groups believed men should collaborate with their female counterparts in order to bring about positive social change which would benefit both men and women (Messner, 1998; Coston & Kimmel, 2013). Men's liberationists founded organisations such as the National Organisation for Men Against Sexism and formed their own parallel critiques of the 'male sex role', such as expectations of men to provide for their family as the sole breadwinner (Messner, 1998; Coston & Kimmel, 2013). According to Messner (1998), such analysis allowed men's liberationists to attract men to feminism by emphasising how they too could benefit from an end to patriarchy. However, this also led to 'strains and tensions' (p. 256) as many men found it difficult to reconcile men's supposed power and privilege with the negative aspects of the male sex role, such as higher male suicide rates, and the role of men as families' main earners. Sex role theory could be used to argue that men were equally oppressed by sexism as women, if not more so.

By the 1970s, a cleavage was beginning to form with the emergence of an anti-feminist men's rights movement. In contrast to pro-feminist men's liberationists, men's rights activists either 'downplayed or angrily disputed' feminist claims that a patriarchal social order oppressed women and privileged men (Messner, 1998, p. 256). Feminism was argued to be a 'hateful ideology' and women's empowerment was seen as the true source of men's misery (Coston & Kimmel, 2013, p. 372). Typical evidence of male oppression included factors such as: male-only military drafts; lower rates of paternal custody arrangements but higher rates of child support and alimony payments; higher rates of male homelessness, suicide and workplace deaths; lack of support for male victims of sexual and domestic violence; and fraudulent accusations of rape and domestic violence (Messner, 1998; Fox, 2004; Coston & Kimmel, 2013). Many of these arguments are reproduced within contemporary men's rights discourse (Schmitz & Kazyak, 2016). Towards the end of the decade, men's rights activists founded their own organisations such as Men's Rights Inc. and National Coalition of Free Men (Messner, 1998). Like feminists and men's liberationists, men's rights activists published positional literature, with key texts (Clatterbaugh, 2000) including *The Masculine Mystique* (Kimbrell, 1997)[2] and *The Myth of Male Power: Why Men are the Disposable Sex* (Farrell, 1993). The latter is particularly noteworthy, given that Warren Farrell had previously identified as a men's liberationist and been hailed as 'the most public male feminist in the USA' (Messner, 1998, p. 262). His career trajectory exemplifies shifts from a discourse of men's liberation to a discourse of men's rights.

Another consequence of the schism was the foundation of a 'mythopoetic' movement, which sought to enable men to search for some 'deep' or 'essential' masculinity thought to have been lost in modern societies (Coston & Kimmel, 2013, p. 371). Robert Bly's *Iron John: A Book about Men* (1990), a key text of the movement (Clatterbaugh, 2000), describes the supposed prevalence of 'soft males' who lacked male role models and consequently had not been properly socialised into masculinity. To solve this perceived problem and help men reclaim their masculinity, mythopoetic leaders organised male-only events such as wilderness retreats, stadium rallies and group therapies (Kimmel & Kaufman, 1994). Just as men's liberationists claimed men could benefit from feminist activism, mythopoets claimed that (heterosexual) women stood to benefit from the mythopoetic movement, as by attending their events men could become more nurturing and emotionally responsive partners (Coston & Kimmel, 2013, p. 371).

---

[2] The title of Kimbrell's (1997) book alludes to Betty Friedan's early feminist text *The Feminine Mystique* (1963).

In contrast to the men's rights movement, the relationship between the mythopoetic movement and feminism was ambivalent. Although feminists and anti-feminists alike praised the movement for encouraging men to open up emotionally, there was also criticism. Some anti-feminists accused mythopoets of promoting femininity rather than masculinity (Fox, 2004), while feminist critiques concerned the movement's gender essentialism and appropriation of Indigenous mythologies and spiritual practices at their rallies (Kimmel & Kaufman, 1994). Fox (2004) also finds that mythopoets were largely unaware of both pro-feminist and anti-feminist men's movements. Instead, mythopoets described themselves as 'largely gender separatists, neither pro-feminist nor anti-feminist' (Kimmel, 2013, pp. 105–6) rather than espousing a more explicitly hostile backlash to feminism.

However, the mythopoetic movement had declined in popularity by the late 1990s (Clatterbaugh, 2000; Fox, 2004). Clatterbaugh (2000) attributes this decline to lack of a long-term strategy and repetitiveness of their writings and gatherings: if a man had attended one mythopoetic rally, there was little need to attend a second. Nevertheless, it did not disappear entirely; for example, the ManKind Project was founded in 1984 and continues to organise 'male initiation' retreats following the ethos of the mythopoetic movement. Moreover, while the mythopoetic movement may have declined, men's rights movements have continued to proliferate with the growth of social media, paralleling shifts towards digitally mediated activism within feminism (Munro, 2013). Between the late 2000s and mid-2010s, a new network of anti-feminist websites and social media accounts started to take shape (Hermansson et al., 2020). Previously established organisations such as the National Coalition for Men created websites and new men's rights organisations were formed, offline and online such as A Voice For Men and Return of Kings (see Kelly, 2020, for an analysis of these sites). As well as their own websites, men's rights groups established a presence on mainstream platforms such as Twitter, Facebook and YouTube.

This network of men's rights blogs, websites and social media is often collectively referred to as the 'manosphere'. Reddit has been singled out as an especially prominent site of activity (Ging, 2019; Ribeiro et al., 2020), which hosts manosphere subreddits such as r/MGTOW and r/TheRedPill (Krendel, 2020). An intertextual reference to the film *The Matrix* (1999), taking the red pill is a metaphor for becoming aware of 'life's ugly truths' such as 'feminism's misandry and brainwashing' (Ging, 2019, p. 640). Conversely, a person who is 'blue-pilled' is thought to live in ignorance and delusion. While this sort of language is common throughout the manosphere, the network is not ideologically or linguistically homogeneous (McGlashan & Krendel, forthcoming 2023). Researchers typically distinguish at least four major groups: men's rights activists; involuntary celibates, also known as incels, who perceive themselves as incapable of finding a romantic partner despite desiring one (Heritage & Koller, 2020); pick-up artists, or PUAs, who share strategies for seducing women (Dayter & Rüdiger, 2022); and Men Going Their Own Way (MGTOW).

MGTOW comprise men who voluntarily abstain from relationships with women, due to their belief that heterosexual relationships and marriage are oppressive for men. Rejecting the breadwinner role, MGTOW encourage each other to 'recentre themselves' and pursue an 'individualistic, self-empowering way of life' (Wright et al., 2020, p. 908). Separatism is often more of a matter of degree, with Lin (2017, p. 90) describing four different stages. At the first level, a man has "taken the red pill" but still desires a wife or girlfriend. At the second level, a man has become aware of the alleged dangers of women and so pursues only casual relationships, avoiding commitments such as marriage, cohabitation or co-parenting. At the third level, a man abstains from short-term relationships and limits any interaction with women. Finally, at the fourth level, a man disengages from society altogether and may even attempt to live off the grid. Men who practice celibacy are referred to within the community as 'monks', while the few who reach level four are known as 'ghosts' (Lin, 2017; Wright et al., 2020). Precise demographics are difficult to obtain, but MGTOW are thought to comprise mostly white, middle-to-upper-class men (Lin, 2017) and at its peak, the MGTOW subreddit had over 145,000 subscribers before it was banned in August 2021. MGTOW Facebook groups and self-hosted forums comprise tens of thousands of members, while MGTOW YouTube channels attract millions of views (Bates, 2020).

The emergence of MGTOW is usually dated to the early 2000s, following the publication of a 'MGTOW manifesto' by two authors writing under the pseudonyms Solaris and Ragnar (Lamoureux, 2015; Bates, 2020). This manifesto was selected as one of the five MGTOW texts for analysis (see Section 4). The MGTOW subreddit was created in 2011 and enjoyed continual growth before surging to prominence in 2017, when it was briefly the most popular and active manosphere subreddit (Ribeiro et al., 2020). However, the subreddit was placed in 'quarantine' in January 2020, meaning that the subreddit and its contents remained online but could only be accessed by users with a Reddit account, and visitors would be greeted with a warning that the subreddit contained 'shocking or highly offensive content'. Reddit administrators did not explain their rationale, but it was speculated that the timing of their intervention related to a recent news story which revealed that a US coast guard officer facing charges of attempted domestic terrorism was a frequent user of r/MGTOW (Owen, 2020; Pedroja, 2021; see chapter 7). Fifteen months later, in August 2021, the subreddit was banned entirely.

Research suggests that, despite its separatist aims, MGTOW discourse has a disproportionate focus on women. For example, Wright et al. (2020) found that women were the primary topic of one third of all MGTOW forum posts, while 59 per cent of posts analysed mentioned women. Jones et al. (2020, pp. 12–4) suggest such a contradictory 'woman-obsessed separatism' is perhaps due to the tensions surrounding what it means to be MGTOW, leading the community to centre around what a man is not doing (dating women) rather than what he is doing. A similar point has been made about lesbian separatism (Dixon, 1988), and our analysis in Section 5 will show that some manifestos feature negative definitions of the in-group.

MGTOW are sometimes conflated with men's rights activists (MRAs). However, the two groups have significant differences. Firstly, they differ in terms of their goals and strategy: while MRAs aim to achieve social change through 'collective protest' and 'social reforms', MGTOW 'focus on self-preservation' and are more individualistic (Wright et al., 2020, p. 910). Secondly, they differ in their structure and organisation. Some MGTOW refute the idea that they constitute a group, let alone a movement (Wright et al., 2020), so there is no MGTOW equivalent to organisations like Men's Right Inc. Finally, they differ in membership: there are several prominent women within the men's rights movement (Kelly, 2020) whereas MGTOW, as the name suggests, is only open to men. Wright et al. (2020, p. 917) describe the so-called 'tuna fishing' activities on the MGTOW forum, where members are encouraged to 'hunt out women and feminised men', who are to be removed from the forum.

In some respects, MGTOW exhibit similarities with the mythopoetic men's movement. Both groups attempt to create homosocial spaces, in either the physical or digital world, and prioritise individualistic self-improvement and reclaiming masculinity as they understand it. Much like the mythopoetic movement, MGTOW are less well-known than both their pro-feminist and manosphere-based contemporaries and, as a result, may be perceived by outsiders as harmless or even making 'valid points' about gender relations (e.g., Boss Hunting, 2019). MGTOW primarily communicate via social media and are heavily reluctant to organise meet-ups in physical space, viewing requests to do so with suspicion (Vivenzi, 2018). Furthermore, while the mythopoetic movement is mostly ambivalent towards feminism (Fox, 2004), MGTOW are virulently anti-feminist (Lin, 2017; Jones et al., 2020; Wright et al., 2020). Overall, MGTOW represent the male separatist faction of the manosphere, valuing sovereignty and independence above all. By separating from women, men are thought to be able to prioritise their own needs and escape from gendered oppression.

We started this section by referring to lesbian separatism as a social movement while calling MGTOW a network. In the next section, we will justify those labels by reviewing the literature on social movements and manifestos.

3 Social Movements and Manifestos

In this section, we will provide some background on social movements as they have been theorised in sociology, including an assessment on whether the two groups we focus on in this Element, lesbian separatists and MGTOW, constitute social movements or not. This will be followed by a review of the mostly discourse analytical literature on manifestos as an important textual tool employed by social movements and other groups.

3.1 Social Movements

Social movements have been defined in various different ways throughout sociological literature (see e.g., Danio, 1992; Snow et al., 2004; Tarrow, 2011; della Porta & Diani, 2020). However, across these various definitions, certain commonalities can be identified, such as a level of organisation, temporal continuity, collective action and collective identity. In this Element, we follow the definition proposed by Snow et al. (2004, p. 11):

> Social movements can be thought of as collectivities acting with some degree of organization and continuity outside of institutional or organizational channels for the purpose of challenging or defending extant authority, whether it is institutionally or culturally based, in the group, organization, society, culture, or world order of which they are a part.

Firstly, the authors describe social movements as 'collectivities', meaning that large numbers of people are involved. Furthermore, the individuals involved must be sufficiently organised and networked together (Danio, 1992). Snow et al. (2004) further explain that social movements exhibit different forms or degrees of organisation, but conclude that all their activities will be organised in some way. Still, neither can social movements be reduced to organisations nor does a single organisation constitute a social movement (Danio, 1992; della Porta & Diani, 2020). Rather, social movement organisations provide the 'resources and opportunities for action to escalate' as well as 'sources for the recreation and production of loyalties and collective identities' (della Porta & Diani, 2020, p. 5).

Members of social movements believe they can achieve more as a collective than they would as individuals, and movements are therefore considered a form of collective action (Snow et al., 2004; Tarrow, 2011; della Porta & Diani, 2020). Broadly speaking, collective action refers to 'any goal-directed activity engaged in jointly by two or more individuals' (Snow et al., 2004, p. 6). Collective action is also associated with 'high levels of organizational resources and formation of collective identities' (Bennett & Segerberg, 2012, p. 739). However, not all forms of collective action are associated with social movements. For instance, Snow et al. (2004) argue that social movements are different from collective behaviours such as 'crowds, panics, fads or crazes' (p. 7), as they require 'some degree of sustained collective action' (Snow et al., 2004, p. 11). Thus, while social movements may make use of methods such as protesting outside a city hall, a single such event would not constitute a social movement. For Tarrow (2011), the collective action involved in a social movement is also of the 'contentious' type, which means that it involves 'interrupting, obstructing or rendering uncertain the activities of others' (p. 9). Snow et al. (2004) claim that social movement activity involves non-institutional forms of collective behaviour, such as marches and rallies. It is the latter point which distinguishes social movements from official special interest groups, as the latter operate primarily within the established political sphere and are regarded as legitimate actors within it, whereas social movements typically occupy a more precarious position (Snow et al., 2004, p. 7). In sum, social movements are typically associated with sustained, contentious and non-institutionalised forms of collective action.

Furthermore, collective identities are said to play an 'essential role' in social movements (Danio, 1992, p. 9). Social movements require members to hold a shared set of beliefs and a shared sense of belonging (Danio, 1992, p. 8), where members come to think of themselves as part of the in-group that is the movement and share a 'common purpose and … commitment to a cause' (della Porta & Diani, 2020, p. 22). In addition to seeing themselves as members of a social movement, participants must also be recognised as such by both those inside and outside of the social movement (Danio, 1992, pp. 8–9).

From the perspective of framing theory, social movements are thought to partake in various 'core framing tasks' which involve the creation of collective action frames. Collective action frames are defined as 'action-oriented sets of beliefs and meanings that inspire and legitimise the activities' of a social movement (Benford & Snow, 2000, p. 614; for a critique of framing as employed in social movement research, see Johnston, 2023). Benford and Snow (2000) highlight three core framing tasks that are of particular relevance: diagnostic framing, prognostic framing and motivational framing. The first core framing task is the creation of 'diagnostic' frames, where it is collectively decided what the problem is that is being opposed. Social movements respond to social, political or cultural problems such as gender inequality or climate change, although smaller-scale or more local issues may also be tackled.

Furthermore, social movements must also collectively decide who is most affected by, and who is to blame for, the social problem in question. Here, social movements create 'injustice frames' in identifying the victims of injustice or 'adversarial frames' in identifying which actors are morally good and which actors are evil (Benford & Snow, 2000, p. 616). This relates to the formation of collective identities, as the creation of such frames allows members to delineate who can and cannot legitimately be considered a member of their social movement and moreover, which groups may be considered an opponent of the social movement. As we shall see in the subsequent analyses (Sections 5 and 6), such role allocation plays a central role in manifestos.

Other core framing tasks include the creation of 'prognostic frames' and 'motivational frames' (Benford & Snow, 2000, pp. 616–7). After diagnosing a social problem, social movements must also prognose a solution and a recommended course of action, or strategy, to tackle the social problem. As previously discussed, some scholars argue that social movements typically pursue their goals via non-institutional means, such as marches, boycotts or sit-ins (Snow et al., 2004). Furthermore, Tarrow (2011, p. 10) suggests that those means could entail more discursive activities, such as the creation of slogans, forms of dress, or recontextualising familiar objects with new symbols. Linguistically speaking, various text and activity types are employed by social movements, including 'personal conversations, informal meetings and assemblies, storytelling, declarations, press releases, advertising, campaigns [and] letters' (van Dijk, 2023, p. 114). Finally, social movements must engage in 'motivational framing' tasks, which entails providing a rationale for engaging in collective action (Benford & Snow, 2000, p. 617). After having proposed a method or course of action, social movement organisers must ensure that its participants remain convinced that the recommended methods are necessary and urgent and must also seek to recruit new members.[3]

Given the above definition, lesbian separatism clearly qualifies as a social movement. As its ethos rejected hierarchies and designated leaders, organisational structures took the form of small and decentralised collectives sharing work and often living spaces. Separatist beliefs and values were communicated through pamphlets and magazines within the movement, as well as by members who travelled between groups. Joining a separatist community required a long-term and possibly indefinite commitment from members; although individual groups might disband after a number of years, separatism as a movement lasted for more than two decades. For separatists, dissociating from men constituted

---

[3] The search to gain new members is encapsulated in what became the slogan of activist group Lesbian Avengers: 'We recruit!'

a form of collective action in itself, but groups also engaged in activities such as publishing, subsistence farming, and making and distributing music.

As for diagnosing the social problem they opposed, lesbian separatists were very clear that male oppression is the root cause of humanity's problems, leading not only to female suffering but also to war, poverty and environmental destruction. Although some Black feminists disagreed with this analysis (see Combahee River Collective, 1977; hooks, 2005), for most separatists, men were clearly identified as being to blame, up to the point where some accounts lament that rather than being woman-centred, some separatist collectives spent 'time and energy . . . in endless discussions on the evils of men' (Dixon, 1988, p. 81). Most scenarios that involve oppressors and victims also feature traitors, and lesbian separatists between them identified a number of secondary others, including hetero- and bisexual women and, for some, trans women as well as liberal feminists. This scenario made for a strong collective identity. The solution to the problem of patriarchy was separatism itself, so that separatists could cast themselves as victims that had become potential saviours. As detailed in Section 2, the movement folded when its members could no longer convince enough women that separatism was a viable and necessary form of collective action to bring down patriarchy.

In contrast, MGTOW cannot be considered a social movement in the same way that lesbian separatists could. Importantly, MGTOW resist the very labelling of themselves as a coherent group in the first place, much less a social movement (Wright et al., 2020). Furthermore, MGTOW emphasise individual sovereignty and personal identities (Wright et al., 2020; Aiston, 2023) as opposed to collective identities. For instance, Aiston (2023) finds that user descriptions of MGTOW emphasise individualism through linguistic choices such as 'self-ownership' and 'you're own boss [*sic*]'. Moreover, MGTOW reject calls for collective action (Wright et al., 2020) and prefer personal action frames. Acts of 'resistance' are more likely to involve individual lifestyle changes and consumer purchases than attending a protest (Aiston, 2023). Discussing the manosphere in general, it has been suggested that the sharing of individual emotional narratives takes precedence over the pursuit of collective action (Ging, 2019; Siapera, 2019).

Therefore, MGTOW is better characterised as an 'affective public' (Papacharissi, 2014, 2016) operating via the logic of 'connective action' (Bennett & Segerberg, 2012) as opposed to a social movement operating via collective action. Papacharissi (2016, p. 311) defines affective publics as 'networked publics that are mobilized and connected, identified, and potentially disconnected through expressions of sentiment', such as storytelling practices. Collective action is distinguished from 'connective action': while collective action is organised on the basis of collective identity and adherence to a collective ideology, connective action is based on the sharing of more personalised action frames, often across social media networks (Bennett & Segerberg, 2012). For connective action, there is little to no formal organisation or coordination of action, and digital media becomes an organising agent instead (Bennett & Segerberg, 2012). Communication therefore centres on personal expressions of individual grievances, assembling 'collaborative but not collective narratives' (Papacharissi, 2016, p. 314). Connective action practices 'permit people to express interest in or allegiance to issues without having to enter into complex negotiation of personal or collective politics' (Papacharissi, 2016, p. 314).

An account of social movements would not be complete without mentioning their problematic aspects. Sternisko et al. (2020) discuss what role conspiracy theories, the belief 'that a powerful group of people are secretly working towards a malevolent or unlawful goal' (p. 1), play in promoting anti-democratic social movements. According to them, social movements become vulnerable to conspiracy theories when members feel a need to increase their personal and collective self-image, to give meaning to their surroundings and to 'feel safe and in control' (p. 3). This suggests that conspiracy theories are more likely to flourish when individuals and groups find themselves confronted with seemingly senseless structures and developments which threaten their positive sense of self, for example, a sudden and severe economic crisis that threatens a decline into poverty. The wish to safeguard one's social identity is crucial in this regard, serving as it does as a motive to accept the contents of a conspiracy theory. This motivation may or may not co-occur with a wish to be special or non-normative as a person or group, which is afforded by 'the structural properties that all conspiracy theories have in common' (Sternisko et al., 2020, p. 2), such as explaining events and building community. Studies in social psychology have shown that it is especially members of a social movement 'who believe in their group's superiority but are anxious about its recognition' who are attracted to conspiracy theories (Sternisko et al., 2020, p. 4). Both lesbian separatists and MGTOW believe that their in-group is better than the so-called 'opposite sex' and better than women and men who do not share their beliefs; both see themselves threatened by the respective out-groups, and both are invested in a non-normative social identity. They are therefore prone to conspiracy theories (see our discussion of references to the 'white genocide' far-right conspiracy theory in the MGTOW data in Section 6). However, unlike social movements like QAnon, it is exactly the separatist nature of the two groups in focus that has prevented either from having a destabilising impact on wider society.

Collective and connective groups alike have an interest in circulating their beliefs and ideas, be that to recruit new members or to reinforce in-group identity. One way of doing so is through manifestos.

3.2 Manifestos

Derived from the Italian, where 'manifesto' describes an inventory (i.e., that which is manifest), the word was originally used in English to denote a decree from an authority and later referred to a tool for a political party or movement and, since the twentieth century, for an artistic movement (OED, 2022). In their political sense, manifestos have been defined in a variety of ways, for instance as 'tools to make public political sentiments and positions' (Colman, 2010, p. 377), as 'a repository of authoritative statement[s] of what the party plans to do in government' (Pearce, 2014, p. 24), and as

> open extensive declarations of individual ideologies for campaigns, comprising small texts in terms of word count but with massive implications for voters' perception of the candidates' political leanings. (Yan Eureka Ho & Crosthwaite, 2018, p. 629)

Most of these definitions centre around manifestos as used by parties in election campaigns and their function as statements of principles and/or intentions.

Others broaden the scope of what a manifesto can contain, as well as who is able to produce a manifesto. Van Dijk (2023, p. 113) advances that party political manifestos would more accurately be called 'programs', as 'manifestos are a prominent discourse genre of protest, resistance and solidarity'. Manifestos can be defined as any 'written summaries of ideologies', whether or not they are associated with a political party (Taub & Hamo, 2011, p. 416). Indeed, the point has been made that 'manifestos of social movements are perhaps the most direct discursive expressions of underlying ideologies' (van Dijk, 2023, p. 116). We here define ideology as a 'network of beliefs that gives rise to expectations, norms and values about events, ideas and people' (Koller, 2014a, p. 239). Alternatively, manifestos have been referred to as 'a declaration of the intentions of the individual or group producing the manifesto' and as oriented towards the future (Pearce, 2014, p. 27). Such summaries and declarations can also signal which topics are important to a group, communicate a group's stance and ideology, and persuade readers to share their vision (Farrukh & Masroor, 2021). Yan Eureka Ho and Crosthwaite (2018) also argue that the aim of a manifesto is to both generate support from existing allies and create new allies. Scarabicchi (2020) broadens the definition of the manifesto to a public statement of beliefs which encourages readers to support a given cause, aims to provide hope to the people it advocates for and fosters social connections between supporters. In less academic terms, Unter and Kelly (2020) maintain that '[a] manifesto should be a grandiose declaration . . . A self serious provocation . . . A call to action. A call for revolutionary change'.

Taub and Hamo (2011) use the term 'manifesto' to describe the writings of the Israeli religious settlers' movement in 1974 and 1980, noting that manifestos have the dual purpose of ensuring homogeneity of beliefs among the in-group and persuading the public to support them. Furthermore, in Kupper and Meloy's (2021) work on terrorist manifestos, all relevant texts were explicitly labelled as manifestos and took a variety of forms, including online posts on social media platforms, websites or forums. Moreover, Scarabicchi (2020) notes in her discussion of three migrant manifestos that manifestos can also be written on behalf of a marginalised group by people external to that group, as a way of showing public support for them.

The above review of the literature demonstrates that although the purposes of different types of manifesto vary, they all share two main aims: to develop a consistent internal worldview within a given group as well as to persuade readers external to the group that this worldview is valid. Manifestos have therefore been analysed in terms of their ideological stance and the topics discussed within them, the way they are structured and the linguistic features which characterise them. Firstly, concerning topics, past literature on political manifestos has investigated a range of concerns, including immigration (Scarabicchi, 2020; van Dijk, 2023, pp. 124–6) and religion (Taub & Hamo, 2011). In terms of discourse structure, manifestos begin with an introductory statement which can include an address from the group leader and/or introduce the group's aims (Aman, 2009; Taub & Hamo, 2011; Pearce, 2014). This introduction is then followed by a statement of the group's principles and goals, which can be accompanied by policies informed by them (Aman, 2009; Taub & Hamo, 2011; Pearce, 2014; Scarabicchi, 2020). Manifestos can also contain critiques of oppositional groups and their policies, if the manifesto is written by a party or group which is not in power, and propose solutions which address these critiques (Pearce, 2014; Szenes, 2021). Alternatively, when the group has been in power for a while, manifestos (or programs) can detail past achievements in a self-promoting fashion (Aman, 2009). Finally, Aman (2009) notes that manifestos finish with a pledge to readers that they will stand by the principles outlined therein and an appeal to readers to support the group. Both Scarabicchi (2020) and Taub and Hamo (2011) also note that manifestos tend to adopt an official and authoritative tone, while Colman (2010, p. 376) refers to their authors as 'people who state their beliefs in the absolute terms of the manifesto form'.

As for the linguistic features of manifestos, both Yan Eureka Ho and Crosthwaite (2018) and Szenes (2021) analyse stance in manifestos by carrying out an appraisal analysis (Martin & White, 2005). The former study found that a generally positive attitude was indexed in the political manifestos by prospective candidates, who discussed their future visions and optimism for Hong Kong. Meanwhile, Szenes (2021) shows how the grievances expressed by the neo-Nazi Nordic Resistance Movement group were framed in terms of negative propriety, whereas the group's proposed solutions to the grievances were ascribed positive propriety. Furthermore, Scarabicchi (2020) observes how support for migrants is communicated through the use of different social actor terms which emphasise humanity and kinship such as 'migrant brothers' and 'fellow human beings'. Absolute quantifiers such as 'all', 'everyone' and 'everywhere' are also used to promote a sense of cross-cultural unity, and the first-person plural 'we' is employed to represent migrants as a community.

In fact, the use of first-person plural pronouns has been identified as a key linguistic feature of manifestos across multiple studies (Taub & Hamo, 2011; Pearce, 2014; Scarabicchi, 2020). For instance, Pearce (2014) found that 'we' and 'our', as well as 'will' and 'to' were key function words in Labour, Conservative and Liberal Democrat UK election manifestos from 1900 to 2010. 'We' was used to establish the beliefs and identity of the political party in constructions – as in 'we believe' –, while 'our' was used inclusively to reference 'our people' and 'our country' as well as to indicate what political parties take as values and topics of interest shared between themselves and the reader. Also, the keyness of 'will' indicates how political manifestos are used to make pledges to the public about future actions.

Following Holland (2014), we adopt a view of the manifesto genre as foundational documents that provide culturally resonant frames and enable social movements.[4] According to Holland (2014), and similar to Benford and Snow's (2000) frames for social movements, manifestos comprise six socio-semantic elements: role allocation, folklore narratives, ethical norms, utopian schemes, strategic planning and motivational appeals. Role allocation involves how personal and group identity is represented and constructed, and how in-groups and out-group roles are allocated. Folklore narratives are used to create a 'comprehensive, mythical worldview' (Holland, 2014, p. 384) of both the in-group and out-group and thus serve to create boundaries between groups. These narratives can be told by the author of a manifesto or expressed through

---

[4] While our discussion of gender-based separatism in this book is based on manifestos as a text type, it should not go unmentioned that all-women societies in particular have been the topic of fictional writing as well. Relevant works range from Charlotte Perkins Gillman's utopian novel *Herland* (1915 [1979]) to various feminist science fiction writings in the latter half of the twentieth century – for example, Joanna Russ's short story *When It Changed* (1972); see also Shugar (1995, pp. 121–148) – and, most recently, Sandra Newman's novel *The Men* (2022).

intertextual references to texts which are culturally salient in the group's history. Ethical norms capture the basic norms and values of the in-group, while utopian schemes encapsulate its ideals. Strategic planning is the most practically oriented of the elements, as it concerns how action is planned within the group. Lastly, motivational appeals are employed by movement leaders to inspire members to take such action.

Although Holland (2014) originally applied his model to the study of political manifestos and speeches, it has also been used to investigate corporate mission statements (Holland & Nichele, 2016). This demonstrates that manifestos also exist outside the political realm. Nevertheless, Holland (2014) created the model within the paradigm of social movement studies and includes it under the remit of the theory of the New Left and the American civil rights movement, along with the breakaway feminist movements that appropriated the manifesto genre from the late 1960s onwards (Pearce, 2009). This suggests that Holland's (2014) model can be applied to social movements beyond political parties, such as the separatist movements and networks discussed in this Element. When used by avant-garde artistic and non-mainstream political movements, manifestos 'want to radically upend and subvert public consciousness . . ., giving voice to those stripped of social and political power' (Fahs, 2020, p. 5). The genre also works inwardly though, ideally fostering in-group cohesion and doing 'community work [in] the ways in which these texts interact with the social order of feminist communities to participate, through discourse, in the movement' (Shugar, 1995, p. xi).

A variety of methodological approaches has been taken in the past literature to investigate manifestos, including corpus linguistics (Pearce, 2014), corpus-assisted critical discourse studies (Yan Eureka Ho & Crosthwaite, 2018), appraisal analysis (Szenes, 2021), and analysis of legitimation strategies (Farrukh & Masroor, 2021). Our own approach is a multilevel qualitative one. In the next section, we introduce our methods of analysis along with the manifestos selected for the purposes of this Element, and discuss the ethical decisions which influenced this selection.

4 Data and Methods

This section serves the purpose of introducing our data sets, elaborating on our selection criteria, ethical considerations and the collection process, and presenting the methods of analysing the data. Those methods combine deductive argumentation analysis with inductive qualitative discourse analysis, where the latter involves three different levels: contents, discourse functions and linguistic features.

4.1 Data Selection and Collection

To compare the language of gender-based separatism, we investigate the language used in ten manifestos: five written by lesbian separatists and five written by MGTOW. All texts were selected to meet the majority of the six 'socio-semantic elements' that Holland (2014) identifies for manifestos (role allocation, folklore narratives, ethical norms, utopian schemes, strategic planning and motivational appeals). At the beginning of Sections 5 and 6, we will detail what linguistic features encode the manifesto characteristics of the texts and hence make them a suitable choice for analysis.

Lesbian separatist texts have been produced and circulated since 1970, starting with the very influential manifesto *The Woman Identified Woman* (Radicalesbians, 1970; see Koller [2008, pp. 48–58] for an analysis). For this group, we have chosen manifestos from different decades, as shown in Table 1.

There is no text for the 2000s, as the idea and strategy of lesbian separatism was at a low ebb then: too much time had elapsed since its heyday but not enough time had passed for a review, let alone a revival. To compensate for this gap, we have included two texts from the late 1990s.

As for the MGTOW manifestos, three were collected from the r/TheRedPill subreddit, which is a subreddit dedicated to discussions about what it means to be a man in a society which is perceived as favouring women over men. Reddit was selected as a data collection site for this study because it has been identified as a popular site for MGTOW in the past literature (e.g., Lin, 2017; Farrell et al., 2019). It should be noted that although a MGTOW subreddit (r/MGTOW) existed at the time of data collection, the subreddit was banned in August 2021 by Reddit for breaking its site-wide content policy, which prohibits content that promotes hate based on identity or vulnerability (Reddit, 2020). Furthermore, although there is a stand-alone website dedicated to discussions of MGTOW beliefs (www.mgtow.com), the website has been unavailable since May 2021. Therefore, the r/TheRedPill subreddit was the site frequented by MGTOW which has been the most consistently accessible and arguably the most public by virtue of being hosted on a popular content aggregation website. This meant that there were fewer ethical issues to consider when using these data.

Three of the five MGTOW texts were selected by searching for posts in r/TheRedPill which showed most of the characteristics of manifestos stipulated by Holland (2014). The selected texts were also tagged by their authors with a 'flair', which is a tagging system on Reddit used to filter content in a given subreddit. The texts from the r/TheRedPill in question were tagged with

Table 1 Details of the lesbian separatist manifestos

Mnemonic	Title	Year	Author(s)	Source	Description
L1	The Furies	1972	Ginny Berson	*The Furies: lesbian/feminist monthly 1*(1), 1 Republished at https://web .archive.org/web/ 20120214120521/http:// www.rainbowhistory.org/ Furies001.pdf	Discusses the Furies as mythological figures and sets out the collective's feelings and goals.
L2	Relating to dyke separatists: Hints for the non-separatist lesbian	1983	Marty, with the help of the dykes of S.E.P.S. (Separatists Enraged, Proud and Strong)	Pamphlet reprinted in Hoagland and Penelope (1988, pp. 95–7) Republished at https://unobject .tumblr.com/post/ 4558118359/relating-to- dyke-separatists-hints-for-the	A bullet point list discussing preconceptions about the movement, addressed to women who are not lesbian separatists.
L3	Some thoughts on separatism	1998	Crow Cohen	www.vtpride.org/may98/crow .htm (defunct)[5]	A recounting of the author's friend questioning her sexuality and the author's emotional response.

---

[5] The two texts from defunct websites are available as scanned copies upon request.

Table 1 (cont.)

Mnemonic	Title	Year	Author(s)	Source	Description
L4	Lesbian separatism?	ca 1998	Fran Friesen	www.intergate.bc.ca/personal/fran/separatism/html (defunct)	The author details her reasons for being a lesbian separatist.
L5	Radical feminism is real feminism	2017	Bev Jo	https://keepingreallesbianfeminismsimple.wordpress.com/2017/08/10/radical-feminism-is-real-feminism-part-1/	Defines radical feminism, with the lesbian separatist movement positioned as an important element.

MGTOW flair, which signalled the posts as being of interest to the MGTOW community in particular. This ensured that the posts collected were representative of the MGTOW community rather than r/TheRedPill as a whole. M1 is the 'MGTOW manifesto' published in 2001 on the blog *No Ma'am* and has been recognised by some as one of the earliest or even the foundational MGTOW text (Lamoureux, 2015; Zuckerberg, 2018; Hermansson et al., 2020). M2 was collected from the r/MGTOW subreddit. An archived link to this post was included on the subreddit sidebar (the 'about' section of a subreddit which describes the community and often includes rules for participation) as recommended reading for new users.

For clarity, the topics of the MGTOW manifestos are described below in Table 2.

Lesbian separatist manifestos present specific ethical issues. Early texts were usually mimeographed and distributed through women's bookshops, festivals and other events or in person between lesbian separatist communities. In line with separatist beliefs, the pamphlets and magazines were intended for a lesbian readership only, sometimes explicitly so. In fact, a later collection of such ephemera (Hoagland & Penelope, 1988) was titled *For Lesbians Only*. However, historical accounts also acknowledge that '[t]he idea of only selling to lesbians presented real, material challenges . . . during the 1970s and . . . the 1980s' (Enszer, 2014, p. 5). Increasing social acceptance, along with the advent of the internet, from the 1990s onwards meant that lesbian (separatist) texts could be distributed more easily but also became available to wider and sometimes unintended audiences: early texts such as L1 and L2 in our data set were scanned and republished online, while the later manifestos (L3, L4 and L5) are original online texts. Such 'remediations of lesbian-feminist work' (Enszer, 2017, p. 63) is double-edged: although 'some aspects of the work by lesbian-feminists are changed, lost and transformed, representation and inclusion in public life has value' (Enszer, 2017, p. 70). In terms of ethics, the fact that all texts could be found on public websites – and, more generally, that lesbian separatists run blogs, Facebook groups and websites – justifies their inclusion in this Element without seeking consent.

As for the MGTOW manifestos, we considered the extent to which these could be considered publicly available. r/TheRedPill has been quarantined (users need to be logged into Reddit and navigate a content warning page to access the subreddit) since September 2018 due to the controversial nature of the community. However, it should be noted that r/TheRedPill do not wish to be quarantined (and thus wish to be more public) and that Reddit's Privacy Policy (Reddit, 2021) indicates that 'much of the information on the Services is public

Table 2 Description of the five MGTOW manifestos

Mnemonic	Author	Year	Title	Source	Description
M1	anonymous (reportedly Solaris & Ragnar)	2001	MGTOW Manifesto	No Ma'Am http://no-maam.blogspot.com/2001/02/mgtow-manifesto.html	Describes the three main goals of MGTOW and strategies for achieving these goals.
M2	MGTOWJayJay	2016	Welcome to MGTOW	r/MGTOW https://archive.ph/xPOqz	Refutes ten common misconceptions about MGTOW, aimed at newcomers.
M3	sir_wankalot_here	2016	The Dangerous Soulmate Myth	r/TheRedPill https://www.reddit.com/r/TheRedPill/comments/4u5wiu/the_dangerous_soulmate_myth/	Critiques the concept of soulmates.
M4	gekkozorz	2017	The Sexodus in action: Millennials are having less sex	r/TheRedPill https://www.reddit.com/r/TheRedPill/comments/4w0ow3/the_sexodus_in_action_millennials_are_having_less/	Discusses the implications of a study which found that millennials are having sexual intercourse less often than previous generations.
M5	animal_one	2020	Why would you want to get married?	r/TheRedPill https://www.reddit.com/r/TheRedPill/comments/j6z24s/why_would_you_want_to_get_married/	Argues that new societal developments such as the welfare state have made marriage obsolete.

and accessible to everyone, even without an account. By using the Services, you are directing us to share this information publicly and freely'. This indicates that the data can be considered suitably public to not require obtaining informed consent. Also, one of the authors reached out to a Reddit administrator on the issue, who stated that obtaining informed consent for using Reddit data was not required.

Furthermore, due to the controversial nature of the MGTOW data, researcher safety needed to be taken into account. Indeed, past literature has characterised the MGTOW community as harassing others in both an active and passive manner (Jones et al., 2020), and so it was important that we minimised any potential security risk to ourselves in the research (British Association for Applied Linguistics, 2021). Massanari (2018) argues that the typical asymmetry in power between researchers and those they research is reversed in the case of potentially dangerous groups, in that the research participants are in a greater position of power than the researchers. This is because the researchers are highly visible to potential harassers, whereas those perpetrating harassment are able to anonymise themselves and appear as an organised group (Massanari, 2018, pp. 3–4). The British Association for Applied Linguistics (2021, p. 5) acknowledges that obtaining informed consent is not necessarily advisable when researching communities who could be potentially hostile towards researchers. Thus, we decided to not seek informed consent from the MGTOW users whose manifestos we used, nor from r/TheRedPill more broadly.

4.2 Methods of Analysis

Two methods of analysis were employed in this research, namely data-led qualitative discourse analysis and deductive argumentation analysis (Reisigl & Wodak, 2016). Firstly, the qualitative discourse analysis involved an investigation of the data that considered how collective identities are constructed in the manifestos. We were interested in how ideologies and identities can be traced via intertextual and interdiscursive references, what discourse functions contributed to specific representations of in-groups and out-groups and what specific linguistic features were employed to realise those functions (Koller, 2012, 2014b). These elements were established inductively to ensure that all relevant features of the specific manifestos were identified.

Considering content brought into a text via intertextuality and interdiscursivity establishes what other texts and genres were referenced in the manifestos, ascertains how authors align with or disalign from others and, importantly, 'reflects on collective identity by showing what features the author borrows to construct that identity' (Koller, 2012, p. 25). In addition to doing identity work, intertextuality and interdiscursivity also reflect authors' ideological norms, values and beliefs, along with the expectations and emotions those give rise to; this is because the voices of others can be integrated into a text in the form of disclaiming or proclaiming (Martin & White, 2005, pp. 117–29). We also identify discourse functions in the texts, as well as the specific linguistic features which realise these discourse functions. For instance, the discourse function of generalising about a group can be realised using multiple linguistic features such as absolute quantifiers ('all', 'every', etc.), numbers and unmodalised statements. We first engaged in a close reading of the data to establish the relevant linguistic features in each manifesto, then analysed those features systematically across the data and finally grouped them into discourse functions. In considering intertextuality, interdiscursivity, discourse functions and linguistic features, we account for the macro (social context), meso (interaction between discourse producers and recipients), and micro (text) levels of discourse, acknowledging that these levels are mutually constitutive (Fairclough, 2010, p. 133).

In addition to the qualitative discourse analysis methods described above, this research also employs methods of argumentation analysis as outlined in the discourse-historical approach (DHA) to critical discourse studies (for further details, see Reisigl, 2014; Reisigl & Wodak, 2016). To analyse the arguments employed within the manifestos, we identified their various *topoi*. Within the DHA, *topoi* are the bridge between a controversial statement in need of justification (also known as a *claim* or a *conclusion*) and its supporting evidence (also known as the *grounds*, *premise* or the *argument*) (Reisigl & Wodak, 2016). They are often realised as causal or conditional paraphrases such as 'if x, then y' (Reisigl, 2014, p. 75). In this analysis, we began with the list of *topoi* provided by Reisigl and Wodak (2001) in their study of discourse on immigration, although not all of their *topoi* were relevant in this research due to the differences in discourse topic. Table 3 details the list of *topoi* operationalised within this study.

By undertaking this analysis, we sought to characterise the manifestos in terms of the identities constructed and the ideologies reflected in them, the discourse functions of representing in-groups and out-groups, and the linguistic features employed to realise those functions. We also determined how similar or different the expression of separatist beliefs are across two groups which both seek to withdraw from what they perceive to be the oppressive gender in wider society. In the next section, we will first present our findings for lesbian separatist manifestos.

Table 3 Selected *topoi* (adapted from Reisigl & Wodak, 2001, pp. 75–80)

Topos	Paraphrase
Advantage	If an action will help us to achieve our goals, then it should be carried out.
Authority	If an authority figure says that an action should (not) be carried out, then it should (not) be carried out.
Definition	If a person, action or thing is named as X, then it should carry the traits or qualities contained in the (literal) meaning of X.
Disadvantage	If an action will not help us to achieve our goals, then it should not be carried out.
Finance	If an action is too expensive or leads to a loss in revenue, then we should try to diminish the costs or avoid the loss.
Freedom	If an action impinges on someone else's freedom, it should not be carried out / if an action enables an individual or a group more freedom, it should be carried out.
History	If the current situation is similar to a previous historical situation, then we should apply the lessons learnt from history and deal with the situation in a similar or different manner.
Humanitarianism	If an action does (not) conform with humanitarian values, it should (not) be carried out.
Responsibility	If a certain group is responsible for the emergence of a problem, then that group should be responsible for the solution.
Threat	If an action will lead to dangerous consequences, then it should not be carried out.

5 Analysis: Lesbian Separatist Manifestos

We start our empirical investigation into the language of gender-based separatism with the analysis of five lesbian separatist manifestos spanning a period of forty-five years, from 1972 to 2017. As detailed in Sections 3 and 4, we have selected the five texts because they meet most of the criteria of manifestos as a genre, containing role allocation, folk narratives, ethical norms, utopian schemes, strategic planning and motivational appeals. Table 4 provides an overview of what manifesto characteristics are included in each of the five lesbian separatist texts, with selected examples.

Table 4 Manifesto characteristics of the lesbian separatist texts

	L1	L2	L3	L4	L5
Role allocations			See sub-sections 5.2 to 5.4		
Folklore narratives	The story of the Furies is the story of strong, powerful women.	Most lesbians in one way or another have been the targets of male assault and sexual crimes.	We had . . . our own newspaper where we gathered and argued and attempted to extricate the dominant culture from every little corner of our lives.	n/a	Acknowledging and fighting all oppression among us has been an integral part of Lesbian Feminism from the beginning.
Ethical norms	Lesbianism is . . . a . . . political choice which every woman must make if she is to . . . end male supremacy.	n/a	Don't you appreciate the solidarity, strength and pride we've achieved in three decades of struggle since Stonewall?	I see lesbian separatism as being about giving my energy to lesbians, and lesbian concerns.	Radical Feminists have no leaders, no stars, no hierarchies.
Utopian schemes	We want to build a movement which makes all people free.	We do not . . . have to . . . want men in our lives in order to fight for a world free of . . . oppressions.	Who knows what a vastly improved world we could create with all that freedom on the loose!	Lesbian only spaces are necessary for me . . . to be in a place that is free from male 'energy'.	Radical Feminism frees us from that mess [patriarchy].

Strategic planning	Our ideology forms the basis for developing long-range strategies and short-term tactics, projects, and actions.	It is impossible for any total 'revolutionary' change to happen while womyn remain allied to men.	We had to swing that pendulum way over to the 'other side' so we could work up the momentum to fight back.	The more I'm in all lesbian space . . . the more I work to create it for myself and others.	If differences in power aren't fought, then the status quo power structure that men set up continues among us.
Motivational appeals	We welcome your comments, letters, articles, fiction, poetry, news, graphics, and support.	n/a	We are forging a Revolution out here. Come join!	You are welcome to join me.	If you've been drawn to feminism but still feel like an outsider because you are seeing some of the same . . . crap that is in the rest of patriarchy, know that that is not true Radical Feminism.

While role allocation will be dealt with in detail in the following sub-sections, Table 4 shows the different linguistic forms that the manifesto characteristics take in the texts. Folklore narratives are realised either by narrative introductions (L1; see also Radicalesbians, 1970) or by past tenses and temporal adverbials. The earliest of the manifestos we analyse, written by The Furies collective, illustrates the observation that

> radical feminist writing in the early stage of the Women's Liberation
> Movement is replete with metaphors and stories of origins; with references
> to goddesses, Amazons, and matriarchy; and with narratives about the cause
> of women's oppression. (Wright, 2004, p. 127)

It is noteworthy that one text from the 1990s (L3) and the text from the 2010s (L5) use narratives to look back on the history and development of lesbian separatism, acknowledging mistakes in the past (L3; e.g., 'we were quite intolerant back then of women who found themselves on the fringes of our community') or lamenting the demise of the movement (L5; e.g., 'Once, feminists were dedicated to unlearning all male lies, but that's part of what we lost'). From manifesto L3 onwards, stories are also told about the writer herself, a notable shift away from a purely collective voice.

The second characteristic, ethical norms, can be difficult to distinguish from utopian schemes: after all, norms and values inform what is seen as desirable and hence the end goal of the movement's efforts. Nevertheless, we can identify some distinct linguistic features for both in the manifestos. For ethical norms, these are lexical items that encode positive values, deontic modality indicating what needs to be done and relational processes defining the social movement. The most recent manifesto also uses a number of negations to clarify what beliefs and practices are at odds with lesbian separatism. Such negation can be seen as part of the writer's pushback against what she perceives as the dilution of the movement's norms. By contrast, linguistic realisations of utopian schemes are consistent throughout the decades, mostly taking the form of metaphoric expressions of freedom, sometimes with added positive evaluation.

As shown in Table 4, strategic planning is encoded in a number of linguistic features, ranging from dynamic modality denoting the ability or capacity of actions or abstract entities, to specific lexis, conjunctions of cause and effect, and conditionals. The most recent text again features negation as well; throughout, its author takes a trans-exclusionary stance, regarding the acknowledgement of trans people as men or women as a 'con [that] has been one of the most destructive things done to females and our movement'. It follows that refusing to accept trans people's gender identity is a strategy for the writer to safeguard radical lesbian feminism and its aims. Finally, in most of the manifestos, motivational appeals are a way to strengthen the movement and they are realised as directly addressing the reader, in the form of second-person pronouns and directives.

5.1 Interdiscursivity

Social movements and the manifestos that their members produce are based on specific ideologies. These can be identified by looking at the contents of the respective texts in the form of interdiscursivity and intertextuality (see Section 4). While some interdiscursive features, such as the use of an academic register (realised in a nominal style or fixed phrases), point to some of the writers' background rather than their ideological alignment, other traces are more informative. Thus, the main discourse that is integrated into the lesbian separatist manifestos is that of socialism. Even though their understanding of 'sexism as the primary contradiction . . . differentiated radical feminists from . . . socialist factions of women's liberation' (Shugar, 1995, p. 180), the very use of the phrase 'primary contradiction' or 'primary oppression' (e.g., Hess et al., 1980, p. 127) illustrates the socialist roots of radical feminist and – linked to, but not identical with, it – lesbian separatist ideology. Likewise, repeated references to a 'Revolution' (L3) or '"revolutionary" change' (L2) owe as much to socialist discourse as does 'the classical movement metaphor of struggle' (van Dijk, 2023, p.120) in 'three decades of struggle' (L3) and declaring the movement's aim to be 'smashing capitalism, racism, and imperialism', in short, 'ending all oppressions' (both L1).[6] Ideological alignment is also conveyed by contrasting lesbian separatism with 'the fascist state of male dominance' (L4) and negatively defining lesbian separatists as feminist who are 'not reformist, liberal, mainstream, or right wing' (L5). The ideological commitment to equality for marginalised groups is also demonstrated by frequent references to what we would now call intersectionality. (It should be noted though that the author of L5 perceives the term as 'a later academic dilution of Feminism'.) Apart from the sexual, political and gendered identity as lesbians, the authors of all five manifestos also make reference to ethnicity, class, age, physical (dis)ability, body shape and religious background, usually in the form of lists of social actors (e.g., 'dykes of color', L2), identity facets (e.g., 'class, race, and nationality', L1) or forms of discrimination (e.g., 'imperialism, ableism, fat oppression', L5). Finally, while there are few intertextual references, the fact that she includes

---

[6] To the best of our knowledge, there is no linguistic study on the features of traditional socialist discourse, although some work has been done on hybrid discourses combining socialism/ Marxism with left-wing populism (e.g., Bartley, 2019; Cadalen, 2020). Our claim that the lexis of the manifestos draws on socialist discourse is therefore based on informed intuition. We gratefully acknowledge Steve Strudwick's help with the literature search on this point.

a quote from Radicalesbians' foundational manifesto *The Woman Identified Woman* (1970) aligns the author of L4 with separatist ideology.[7]

Having discussed the manifesto characteristics of the five texts as well as their authors' ideological affiliations, we will in the remainder of this section present our analysis of how the in-group, lesbian separatists, and different out-groups (men, other women and other feminists) are constructed. We will draw on both qualitative discourse and argumentation analysis to show how role allocation is realised through various language features. The section will close with a brief summary.

5.2 Inter-Group Dynamics

The analysis in this sub-section will show how the manifesto writers establish in-groups and out-groups and represent them as both homogenous and diametrically opposed to each other.

5.2.1 Generalising about Groups

There is a clear construction of an in-group in contrast to different out-groups in the texts, and the groups are also represented as homogeneous. Linguistically, this is achieved by the use of absolute quantifiers, vague and pseudo-quantifiers and unmodalised statements.

(5.01) Do not conclude that a separatist should 'work through her anger at her father/brother ... ' (or *any* other males of *any* age at *any* time in her life) (L2, original emphasis)

(5.02) I see very few straight women ... being politically involved in fighting/ confronting lesbo hate. (L4)

(5.03) Of course males are our oppressors. (L5)

In all three examples above, the proposition is intensified, be that through the use of italics, adverbs or adverbials. Although the data we selected do not homogenise groups by referring to prototypical members in the singular – as does the author of M3 (see Section 6) – the authors of what is arguably 'the most famous of lesbian separatist manifestos' (Jeffreys, 1990, p. 290) do:

> What is a lesbian? A lesbian is the rage of all women condensed to the point of explosion. She is the woman who ... acts in accordance with her inner

---

[7] The author of L5 includes a number of web links in her text to provide evidence for her claims. However, the fact that most of those links are either broken, have been deleted by their authors or suspended by the hosting company for violation of terms and conditions suggests that integrating links to increase credibility can also backfire.

compulsion to be a more complete and freer human being than her society . . . cares to allow her. (Radicalesbians, 1970)

This view of social groups as not only opposed to each other but also monolithic means that every representative of a relevant group metonymically stands for the whole group. In the case of in-group members, lesbian separatists, this has the effect that individuals are expected to embody the positive norms and values of the whole group. Any deviation therefore becomes a threat to the collective ideology and identity, and it is thus no surprise that discussions about who is and is not – indeed can and cannot – be a lesbian separatist are prominent across the manifestos.

To argue about who can, and who cannot, have legitimate access to women's or lesbian-only spaces, writers use the *topos of definition* in the manifestos. The texts typically argue that the only legitimate participants in lesbian separatism are women and thus, men and boys should not be allowed entrance to women's or lesbian spaces. For example, L2 argues that any 'womyn-only' space that allows young male children to enter is a misnomer and would be insufficient for lesbian separatists' needs.

(5.04) Do not assume that an occasional womyn-only event should be plenty to satisfy separatists' need. For one thing, most so-called 'womyn-only' events actually include boys. Being young, small, and dominated by adults' power does not make a boy female! (L2)

The definitions of 'male' and 'female' that are used to delineate who has legitimate access to women's spaces are fixed and biologically determined. Thus, trans women are defined within the manifestos as 'male', regardless of self-identification or stage of transition. Likewise, 'radical feminists' as a group can be defined according to their beliefs about trans women (but see Section 8). According to L5, radical feminists would 'never genuflect to the trans cult line that men can be women' nor would they ever use terms like 'lesbian' or use she/her pronouns to refer to a trans women because by their definition, such language can only refer to a biological female. In addition to this *topos of definition,* L5 also employs a *topos of justice* to compare transgender women to 'trans-paraplegic' or 'trans-racial' people, or even 'trans-species' people. It is argued that because the concept of changing race or species would be perceived as 'ridiculous', so should the concept of changing gender or sex. Overall, beliefs about gender transition can be used to define who can and who cannot be a radical or lesbian feminist. Consequently, cis women who support trans women are part of a secondary out-group (discussed further in 5.4.2).

After having used a *topos of definition* to define who can and cannot be included within a group, a manifesto author may use a different topos in order to make an argument or generalisation about that group. For example, L4 endorses a quote from the manifesto *The Woman Identified Woman* (Radicalesbians, 1970) to combine *a topos of definition* with *a topos of responsibility*. First, a categorical argument is presented: if one is a man or a straight woman, then by definition one has either direct or indirect male privilege. After having established these binary categories, the manifesto uses *a topos of responsibility* to argue that privileged groups can either choose to uphold oppressive systems of male supremacy and perceived sexual, economic and spiritual slavery of all women, or they can choose to fight against it; there can be no middle ground between these two options. A reader is likely to infer that the latter is the preferred choice and may conclude that because privileged groups are responsible for these problems, they should be held accountable for finding the solutions.

(5.05) Either you are a man or a woman; either you have male privilege or you don't; either you get benefits from that privilege as a straight woman, or you don't. . . . Thus, either you are fighting for an end to male supremacy, or you are responsible for upholding that system (Radicalesbians, 1970; quoted in L4).

5.2.2 Creating an Us-vs-Them Dichotomy

Having been established as homogeneous, the in-group is set in contrast to primary and secondary out-groups, where the primary out-group is men, while women who relate to men in one way or another are a secondary out-group. The latter group includes various social actors, from hetero- and bisexual women to non-separatist lesbians, and is also dynamically positioned: when the focus is on the primary out-group, women are homogenised as victims and/or survivors of male aggression. However, when lesbian separatists emphasise their own identity and goals, the secondary out-groups become multifaceted.

(5.06) The need for lesbian space is not built on a politics of oppression or exclusion of other groups. I have heard it said that lesbians who demand lesbian only space are oppressing other groups who might wish to belong e.g., MTF transgenders, straight women, even men. (L4)

A range of metaphors helps to reinforce the differences between in-group and out-groups, including spatial metaphors:

(5.07) the . . . differences between females and males are obvious (L5)

The inequality between in-group and out-groups is expressed with an intensified FORCE metaphor, even if the actor exerting the force is backgrounded:

(5.08) It is a system in which heterosexuality is rigidly <u>enforced</u> and Lesbianism rigidly <u>suppressed</u>. (L1)

However, it is VIOLENCE metaphors that are most frequently used to construct differences and conflict between groups, chiefly but not exclusively between the in-group and the primary out-group, men. These metaphors may well be topic-triggered, that is, motivated by literal male violence against women.

(5.09) Radical Feminism means recognizing that patriarchy, and males as a group, being at <u>war</u> with the earth and all females. (L5)

(5.10) The crimes that men and boys have committed against womyn and girls are inhuman, horrendous and unforgivable. We name our <u>enemy</u> accordingly. (L2)

(5.11) I see many lesbians at the <u>forefront</u> of the feminist movement, <u>fighting</u> for the rights of straight women. (L4)

(5.12) I have the right to <u>defend</u> my life and our community from the constant <u>attacks</u> on us. (L5)

A more subtle way of constructing in-group vs out-group dichotomies is to directly address out-group members. In fact, the macro-structure of the L2 manifesto is built on this principle, with both the in-group and the secondary out-group named in the title of the text ('Relating to dyke separatists: hints for the non-separatist lesbian'). The body of the text is a bullet-point list of directives and questions, in which the writers ask an imagined out-group member to refrain from certain assumptions, avoid particular utterances and take corrective action. For example:

(5.13) <u>Are you</u> 'sick and tired' of hearing separatists' anger and grievances? <u>Don't put</u> your annoyance on us. <u>Talk</u> with other non-separatists, <u>look at</u> why you're threatened. (L2)

Along with such unmitigated directives, the fact that the title of the L2 manifesto puts the in-group in the plural and the out-group member in the singular suggests that the writers are seeking to reverse the power asymmetry between themselves and the secondary out-group. That other texts from the same period (e.g., Leeds Revolutionary Feminists, 1979; Trebilcot, 1986) were also written in reply to criticism from within the lesbian feminist movement further suggests that there was conflict but also dialogue between the in-group and the secondary out-group of other feminists at the time.

In the following sub-section, we will focus our analysis on the discursive representation of the in-group.

5.3 In-Group

The in-group is represented positively, but we will see in the following that some of that evaluation is modified. The writers construct the in-group as fighters, but to the extent that they are also represented as powerless, lesbian separatists are additionally cast as victims.

5.3.1 Positively Representing the In-Group

Unsurprisingly, the in-group of lesbian separatists is evaluated positively by the authors of the text, often explicitly so.

(5.14) 'Don't you appreciate the solidarity, strength and pride we've achieved?' (L3)

(5.15) Radical Feminists discuss with respect and kindness and caring. (L5)

However, there are also a number of instances in which such positive evaluation is mitigated, be that through adverbs expressing dynamic modality ('potentially') or through counterfactuals.

(5.16) [L]esbianism is potentially an ultimate act of liberation for any woman who dares. Who knows what a vastly improved world we could create with all that freedom on the loose! (L3)

More subtly, mitigation is also present when writers refer to their wishes and potential rather than actions.

(5.17) We want to build a movement which makes all people free. (L1)

(5.18) together we have the strength and courage to take the risks and make the choices (L5)

The *topos of advantage* is used within the manifestos to argue that women should become lesbian separatists because it is to their benefit. L1 and L3 uses a *pro bono publicum* variant of the *topos of advantage* in order to highlight how lesbian separatism can create a 'vastly improved world' (example 5.16), while L1 mentions that lesbian separatism can benefit 'all people' (example 5.17). Furthermore, L1 and L3 also use a *topos of freedom* in arguing that lesbian separatism will bring about freedom (examples 5.16 and 5.17) in addition to a *topos of humanitarianism* to argue that lesbian separatism is a 'Revolution' which can 'effectively stop' oppression and 'male supremacy.'

(5.19) We are forging a <u>Revolution</u> out here. Come join! (L3)

(5.20) We want to build a movement in this country and in the world which can <u>effectively stop the violent, sick, oppressive acts of male supremacy</u>. (L1)

As shown in example 5.19, women readers are encouraged to join lesbian separatists in order to realise these humanitarian goals.

Alternatively, the authors of L3 and L4 employ the *pro bono nobis* version of this topos in order to highlight the benefits for both the in-group and the individual lesbian separatist. These individual benefits are emphasised through use of first-person pronouns, singular nouns and reflexives. Lesbian separatism and lesbian spaces are also described using positive stance participles and adjectives (e.g., 'stimulated', 'vastly improved', 'creative', 'positive'), which emphasise the benefits to women's physical and mental wellbeing of becoming a lesbian separatist. Moreover, L3 uses an extreme case formulation when describing how long these benefits will last ('the rest of your life'). Women readers are to join the lesbian separatist movement in order to reap these purported benefits and improve their individual lives.

(5.21) Coming out as a dyke is potentially the most profound act of <u>self-love</u> <u>a woman</u> can choose. Not only that, by devoting yourself to building lesbian culture you can keep <u>yourself</u> stimulated (intellectually and otherwise) for <u>the rest of your life</u>. (L3)

(5.22) So for all these reasons and many more, I see lesbian separatism as being about giving my energy to lesbians, and lesbian concerns, which means also <u>putting energy into myself, living in creative, lesbian positive environments</u>. You are welcome to join me. (L4)

5.3.2 Creating In-Group Cohesion

To further their objectives, social movements rely if not on uniformity then at least on a cohesive in-group. It is therefore no surprise that the lesbian separatist manifestos include a number of linguistic features to create such cohesion. This can take the form of using in-group terms for self-reference, for example, reclaiming the term 'dyke' (see example 5.21). In the 1980s text (but not in the earliest manifesto), we also find alternative spellings of the words 'woman' or 'women', to exclude the 'man/men' morphemes of the words.

(5.23) Most <u>womyn</u> are survivors of men's rape and abuse (L2)

This feature can only be found as a historical reference in L3 though ('we had ... frequent <u>wimmin</u>-only dances') and not at all in L4. The author of L5 even rejects the spelling practice, stating that 'I don't mean we make trivial changes like changing the spelling of women'. Other ways to refer to the in-group include capitalising the words 'Lesbian(s)' and 'Lesbianism', either consistently (L1, L5) or occasionally (L4). This spelling practice can be seen as a parallel to capital-B 'Black', which was first introduced as part of the US civil rights movement of the late 1960s and 'suggests a shared culture of struggle' (Beckerman, 2021). Another parallel is the use of kinship terms for members of the in-group.

(5.24) I remember how I felt the first time I heard one of those truly kind-hearted <u>sisters</u> (L3)

The in-group is further represented in terms of what its members do, even if the material actions they are said to be engaging in are metaphorical:

(5.25) [B]y devoting yourself to <u>building</u> lesbian culture you can keep yourself stimulated (intellectually and otherwise) for the rest of your life (L3)

The metaphor here can be 'categorized as part of the important Action [element] of manifestos, of course inherently related to its goals' (van Dijk, 2023, p. 120). In-group cohesion can also be achieved by use of the first-person plural pronoun ('we'). Corroborating the observation (see 5.1.2) that the in-group is constructed as homogenous vis-à-vis the primary out-group but as more heterogeneous in contrast to secondary out-groups, authors use an inclusive 'we' to refer to women but an exclusive 'we' to refer to lesbian separatists.

(5.26) <u>We</u> are angry because we are oppressed by male supremacy. (L1)

(5.27) Separatists live with the added oppression of judgement ... when <u>we</u> are out about hating men. (L2)

Use of an exclusive 'we' is often combined with ascribing affect, stance and volition to the in-group. This serves to create in-group cohesion by encoding some of the building blocks of ideology, such as norms and values, along with the goals and emotions that they give rise to.

(5.28) I am a separatist because I <u>believe</u> in a women centered, woman identified, particularly Lesbian defined feminism. (L4)

(5.29) We <u>oppose</u> any dilutions of feminism. (L5)

(5.30) We <u>want</u> to build a movement in this country (L1)

Lesbian separatists also create in-group cohesion through *the topos of authority*. Rather than appeal to external authoritative sources such as laws or elite figures, however, the manifesto writers appeal to their own internal authority, which results from their identity as lesbians and from their past experiences. The data thus illustrate that 'manifesto writers *perform* authority – establishing themselves as speakers, insisting ... that their voice has an audience' (Fahs, 2020, p. 10, original emphasis). In some cases, this may conversely mean that the authority of others is undermined. For example, L2 refutes advice given by therapists on the basis that only lesbian separatists can know what is best for themselves. The author presents lesbian separatist knowledge as authoritative and suggests that external groups should not interfere with, or try to speak over, lesbian separatists.

(5.31) Especially for therapists and counselors: Do not conclude that a separatist should 'work through her anger at her father/brother/son/uncle/ex-husband/grandfather/stepfather (or *any* other males of *any* age at *any* time in her life) in order to let go of her rage and integrate men into her life'. This attitude is a very condescending power trip that says separatists can't know what's best for our growth and survival. (L2, original emphasis)

L5 likewise uses a *topos of authority*. However, in contrast to the above example, the author's internal authority derives from her past experiences and achievements rather than her identity as a lesbian. The author points out that she has been a radical feminist since the movement's inception and in fact 'helped create' the movement itself.

(5.32) I've been a Radical Feminist with no selling out and no diluting or flipping my politics for longer than anyone else I know. That doesn't mean I'm the only one, but considering that I helped create Radical Lesbian Feminism and am still here, I have the right to defend my life and our community from the constant attacks on us. (L5)

This personal experience makes her an authority figure on the subject of radical feminism, and she therefore has the right to define what radical feminism is and, importantly, what it is not.

5.3.3 Representing the In-group as Powerless

We have seen above that some writers intend to reverse the power difference between their in-group and various out-groups. However, some authors also emphasise the marginalised status of the lesbian separatist in-group by representing it as powerless. This is done via a number of grammatical and lexical features, including agentless passives, relational processes of having and being, and explicit references to discrimination, abuse and violence.

(5.33) We are working to change this system which has <u>kept us</u> separate and powerless for so long. (L1)

(5.34) We <u>do not have</u> the power, economic or political resources to oppress other groups. (L4)

(5.35) Lesbians, as <u>outcasts</u> from every culture but their own, have the most to gain by ending race, class, and national supremacy within their own ranks. (L1)

Conversely, the writers of L1 seem to regard the agentive violence of their mythical namesakes with admiration:

(5.36) The story of the Furies is the story of strong, powerful women, the 'Angry Ones', the avengers of matricide, the protectors of women. . . . The Furies tormented Orestes; they literally drove him crazy. (L1)

Overall though, the positive evaluation of the in-group prevails. In the next section, we will focus on how the primary and secondary out-groups are represented in the manifestos.

5.4 Out-Groups

As has become clear from the previous sections, the lesbian separatist manifestos construct both a primary out-group and a number of secondary out-groups. While anyone who was assigned male at birth (including trans women) is seen as part of the primary out-group, secondary out-groups are differentiated in contrast to the in-group, comprising women who are in any way involved with men. In a scenario where lesbian separatists are fighters and sometimes victims, men are cast as oppressors, while members of the secondary out-groups are perceived as collaborators.

5.4.1 Men

Both men as a group and male supremacy as a system are evaluated in exclusively negative terms, often explicitly so. There is a clear pattern of men being represented as acting in harmful ways towards women, but we can also observe some slippage between concrete people and their actions on the one hand and abstract concepts and nominalised actions that background social actors on the other.

(5.37) <u>They</u> [men] <u>suck</u> our energy and then <u>spit</u> us out. (L4)

(5.38) <u>Men</u> still <u>rape</u> and <u>kill</u> us and aren't held accountable. (L5)

(5.39) <u>Patriarchy</u> is built on <u>female-hating</u>, <u>rape</u>, and <u>gynocide</u>. (L5)

(5.40) In order to get out from under <u>male domination</u> which had/has our bodies and minds in a vice grip ever since 'the dawn of mankind' we had to swing that pendulum way over to the 'other side' (L3)

Men are not only abstracted, which reflects an academic register, but occasionally also dehumanised by dint of metonymically being referred to as 'pricks' (L2).

Writers also narrate men's speech acts and ascribe negative feelings and wishes targeted at women to them:

(5.41) Apollo <u>defended</u> Orestes and totally <u>denied</u> the importance of motherhood, <u>claiming</u> that women were no more than passive sperm receptacles for men. (L1)[8]

(5.42) our oppressors . . . have <u>hated</u> . . . us in every culture in patriarchal history (L4)

(5.43) the misogynist world we live in <u>wants</u> us silent and dead (L5)

In terms of argumentation, manifesto writers use the *topos of threat* in order to argue that men pose a danger to women and that consequently, it is legitimate for women to separate from men and hold men in disdain. For example, L2 uses a *topos of definition in* combination with *a topos of threat* to argue that if someone is male, he can legitimately be considered a threat to women. All men are perceived as having the capacity to threaten and violate women, including men who occupy less powerful positions in society such as children and gay men. Therefore, the authors consider it wrong to try and defend men or consider some men to be different: to be a lesbian separatist, one must separate from all men without exception.

(5.44) Do not tell a separatist 'Yeah I hate men too except for my father/brother/ son/cousin/ex-husband/faggot friend . . . He's really an exception, he's really okay.' She doesn't want to hear about him or how you like him! Every male who has violated a female was loved and nurtured by some womon somewhere who thought of him as special. (L2)

---

[8] The ascribed view of women as sperm receptacles is echoed, albeit more crudely, in the term 'cum dumpster', which is used to refer to women across different communities in the manosphere.

A *topos of definition* is also used in L2 in order to justify the derogatory labelling of out-groups. Because men's actions against women are 'extreme and horrendous', it is acceptable and appropriate for lesbian separatists to use 'extreme' or 'horrendous' language when metonymically referring to men.

(5.45) Do not protest in dismay or horror when we say pricks/puds/smegma/
        _____ for whom are commonly referred to as men & boys. Maybe you
        think these terms are 'inhuman,' 'extreme,' 'horrendous,' unfair.' The
        crimes that men and boys have committed against womyn and girls are
        inhuman, horrendous and unforgivable. We name our enemy accordingly.
        (L2)

Furthermore, L4 uses the *topos of history* and the *topos of justice* to argue that lesbian separatists should not have to go out of their way to help out-groups. The author refers to real-life historical examples of the AIDS liberation movement, the 'transgendered movement' and the feminist movement and the lessons learnt from these examples. According to L4, lesbians have historically collaborated with other marginalised groups such as gay men and trans people, but these groups have never returned the favour. These out-groups are thus represented negatively, as selfishly exploiting the labour of lesbians and reinforcing patriarchal gender stereotypes of women as caregivers. The author does not argue that lesbian separatists must *never* collaborate with other social movements. Instead, the argument is that lesbians should not dedicate their whole life or all of their energy to other social movements who would not do the same for them.

(5.46) Separatism does not exclude the possibility of working in coalition with
        other groups on common ground of our oppression. But I will not do that
        at my expense ... I have seen this happen with the gay liberation
        movement, with the AIDS movement, with the transgendered
        movement, where lesbian energy is used to further the cause of
        everyone except the lesbians. (L4)

5.4.2 Other Women

As mentioned above, the lesbian separatist writers in our data also construct a number of secondary out-groups, including women who relate to men. Here we find both less explicit negative evaluation ('token woman', L1) and intensification or hyperbole ('putting up day in and day out with other womyn ... defending men and boys to us everywhere we go', L2). The most recent manifesto uses religious metaphors to delegitimise activists for trans rights as misguided and possibly dangerous and to deny trans women their gender identity:

(5.47) Radical Feminists do not <u>proselytize</u> for men ... Radical Feminists never <u>genuflect</u> to the trans <u>cult</u> line that men can be women or Lesbians. (L5)

We saw in 5.4.1 that men were dehumanised through metonymic reference to them in terms of body parts. In the most recent manifesto, trans women – whom the author sees as men – are dehumanised through metaphor:

(5.48) I object to our Radical Feminist movement and culture being ... <u>parasitized</u> ... . I object when men do it, claiming to be Radical Feminists and demanding we accept them as women. (L5)

Representing out-group members as parasites (see also Frye, 1978, p. 33) echoes the dehumanisation found in anti-Semitic and racist discourses, including 'the genocidal Nazi propaganda against Jewish people and other minorities' (Musolff, 2014, p. 220). Although the manifesto author does not explicitly call trans women parasites, she ascribes the action of 'parasitising' to them, thus coming close to a fascist conceptualisation of that out-group.

However, the most frequent way of negatively presenting the secondary out-group of women who relate to men is by ascribing hypothetical speech, thoughts and feelings to them, in order to refute them. It is impossible to say if those ascriptions are a strawman argument or reports of actual interactions, but it is noteworthy that there is a whole manifesto (L2) that is structured in the form of an imagined or re-enacted dialogue. Other writers use similar language features, too.

(5.49) [D]on't <u>assume</u> her separatism comes out of her being <u>'controlled by her victimization'</u> (L2)

(5.50) I have <u>heard it said</u> that lesbians who demand lesbian only space are oppressing other groups who might wish to belong e.g., MTF transgenders, straight women, even men. (L4)

Although the author of L4 acknowledges 'common ground' between straight women and lesbians, as both groups experience sexism, straight women are also presented as exploiting the labour of lesbians and refusing to fight for lesbian rights. As in example 5.46, *a topos of justice* is used in L4 to highlight this double standard and argue that lesbians should not have to fight for straight women if straight women would not reciprocate (see also example 5.51). Similarly, L1 uses a *topos of threat* to argue that lesbians must 'get out' of heterosexual women's spaces in order to minimise their risk of oppression and dismissal (see example 5.52). L1 also uses a *topos of disadvantage* to argue that it would be impractical for lesbians to form alliances and develop a 'common politics' with straight women, as this will not help lesbians achieve their goals of ending male supremacy.

(5.51) I see many lesbians at the forefront of the feminist movement, fighting for the rights of straight women to live free from the violence of their male partners . . . but I see very few straight women supporting lesbians in battering relationships (L4).

(5.52) Lesbians must get out of the straight women's movement and form their own movement in order to be taken seriously, to stop straight women from oppressing us, and to force straight women to deal with their own Lesbianism. Lesbians cannot develop a common politics with women who do not accept Lesbianism as a political issue. (L1)

5.4.3 Other Feminists

Despite the obvious overlap between other women and other feminists as secondary out-groups, some passages in the manifestos specifically represent the latter, and again their representation is exclusively negative. The author of L5 extends her objection to radical feminism being 'appropriated, parasitized, and gutted' by 'women [with a] distorted version of Radical Feminism'. At the other end of the timeline for our data, The Furies manifesto dehumanises both men and non-separatist feminists through a metaphor scenario in which the latter are the 'prey' of the former, who are referred to in abstract terms:

(5.53) For too long, women in the Movement have fallen <u>prey</u> to the very male propaganda they seek to refute. (L1)

Radical, including separatist, feminists have long sought to set themselves apart from liberal feminists (McAfee & Howard, 2018), so it comes as no surprise to find the following ascribed speech and its refutation in one of the manifestos:

(5.54) Why would I, in these days of . . . liberal <u>thinking</u> of 'we are all one, we are all oppressed, we must all join together, etc . . . ' still announce that I am a separatist. . . . I am a separatist because. (L4)

In the first sentence of her manifesto, the author engages with a question, implicitly ascribed to an unnamed other, that challenges lesbian separatism. Her own stance can be traced in the mocking reference to liberal thinking which takes the form of a list of propositions that are seemingly interchangeable (note the parallelism) and picked at random ('etc . . . '). The tone changes to a more serious one when she gives reasons for her separatist politics and identity.

As discussed in Section 5.4, the manifestos consistently refer to trans women as men or males and so exclude them from the in-group. Furthermore, L5 constructs trans-inclusive feminists as another secondary out-group due to their different perspective. According to the author, there is a sexual threat posed by the main out-group ('men perving on us'), but also an internal threat posed by the secondary out-group who fail to protect the in-group and 'shove' the out-group down their 'throats'. (The VIOLENCE metaphor here has sexual overtones.) Finally, the author also perceives an existential threat to the in-group, as women and feminism risk being made invisible again.

(5.55) In the past, feminists protected each other from male intrusion. Now, when we try to meet, whether in person or online, we are diverted by men perving on us, and by the women who help shove them down our throats. Even worse, <u>feminism and women ourselves are being defined out of existence</u> (L5)

Using a *topos of history*, the author of L5 contrasts the radical feminism of the 1970s with the radical feminism of today, arguing that the same problems persist. Consequently, contemporary feminists must learn from previous mistakes in order to avoid repeating them and thereby pose a threat to the community.

(5.56) Those who do not know history are condemned to repeat it and, even worse, condemn us to repeat it. Those who try to prevent discussion about the past that is relevant to us now are harming our community. (L5)

The discussion of secondary out-groups shows that the manifesto authors carve a very small niche for the in-group, distancing themselves not only from women who relate to men but also from other feminists who hold different beliefs and norms. Notably, the discourse universe of the writers includes no groups that are linked to the in-group. Instead, we find an in-group that is represented as diverse in its demographics but united in its ideology and that is pitted against several equally homogeneous out-groups. The authors realise an ideological square (van Dijk, 1998, pp. 245–9) in that the positive aspects of the in-group and the negative aspects of the out-groups are emphasised, while what is negative about the in-group and positive about the out-groups is suppressed.

The five manifestos span a period of forty-five years and we can therefore observe some diachronic changes in the data set. These include a shift from collective to individual authorship and with it the use of the first-person singular next to first-person plural pronouns from the late 1990s onwards: apparently, later authors are less '[e]namored with the sweeping "we" pronoun' (Fahs, 2020, p. 9) but add their own voice to an imagined unified voice of the movement. Also, narratives of the past move from tracing the (mythical) origin to outlining the development and even decline of lesbian separatism. The reasons for that decline are many, but an important one is the shift from opposing patriarchy as an oppressive system to seeing that system embodied in every male. This role allocation is borne out in all of the five manifestos we analysed in this section, and the point has been made that such 'binary concepts of opposition ... impeded women's abilities to perceive the ways they oppressed other women' (Shugar, 1995, p. 89), for example, women of colour. As Shugar further puts it: 'Construction of a demonic, binary other thus ironically provided the impetus toward female community and made the success of that community impossible' (1995, p. 81). It also prevented coalition-building and gradually narrowed the discursive space for the in-group.

Our second analysis section will investigate five manifestos written by MGTOW as another instance of the language of gender-based separatism.

6 Analysis: Men Going Their Own Way Manifestos

As in Section 5, we begin by outlining the manifesto characteristics found in each of the five MGTOW texts and displaying examples of each characteristic (see Table 5).

Compared to lesbian separatist manifestos, the MGTOW texts contain fewer genre elements. This suggests that because MGTOW do not see themselves as part of a movement, the authors are less invested in producing programmatic texts. Nevertheless, all five texts include at least four out of the six elements identified by Holland (2014) and therefore meet our criteria as manifestos. Folklore narratives in the MGTOW data set are characterised by intertextual references to sources they support (books on gender studies and neuropsychiatry, as well as the far-right media outlet Breitbart). Also, temporal adverbials are used to highlight differences between the past and the present. These sources and temporal constructions are used to justify the arguments being made in the manifestos, namely perceived innate differences between men and women, the impact of feminism in wider society and that MGTOW should not get married.

Ethical norms are established in most of the manifestos by discussing the norms and values of the MGTOW network. There is lexis which denotes both the aims and nature of the group and relational processes which outline the beliefs that in-group members hold. In particular, MGTOW are defined by what they choose not to do, so some statements of ethical norms are negated or contrasted with negatively evaluated beliefs and actions. Interestingly, utopian schemes only occur in M1, realised by using metaphoric expressions of freedom and by constructing and positively evaluating the future scenarios that MGTOW aim to create.

Table 5 Manifesto characteristics of the MGTOW texts

	M1	M2	M3	M4	M5
Role allocations			See Sections 6.2 and 6.3		
Folklore narratives	n/a	n/a	A blog post titled 'The dangerous soulmate myth', *The Manipulated Man* by Esther Vilar and *The Female Brain* by Louann Brizendine	Two Breitbart articles by Milo Yiannopolous	100 years ago men get [*sic*] married because they were forced to, not because they thought it was fun or their duty or a good idea.
Ethical norms	The goal is to instill masculinity in men, femininity in women, and work toward limited government!	A MGTOW has no need for female companionship	[T]he soulmate myth coupled with the fear of growing old alone is extremely dangerous	n/a	Trying to get married today in order to provide a stable household for raising children is a fool's errand.
Utopian schemes	By instilling masculinity in others, as well as yourself, you will actually be improving the lives of everyone, including women and children.	n/a	n/a	n/a	n/a

Table 5 (cont.)

	M1	M2	M3	M4	M5
Strategic planning	PRIME STRATEGIES FOR ACHIEVING OUR GOALS	a MGTOW won't even bother to look in your direction	The solution is to fix yourself first	Don't be a beta weenie.	getting married isn't the way to do it
Motivational appeals	You just go your own way and do what you believe is right.	Welcome to MGTOW. Ready to change your life?	The solution is to fix yourself first	Don't surrender your life to a neurotic cunt who doesn't appreciate you.	n/a

Strategic planning is encoded in all the MGTOW texts by using specific lexis, conditionals constructions which discuss MGTOW actions in hypothetical situations and also negations referring to inaction. Furthermore, the nature of this planning changes over time: whereas M1 presents group strategies for improvements and calls to action via directives, later manifestos present actions to be taken as individualist solutions. This indicates a shift from a more collectivist in-group in the early 2000s, perhaps akin to the mythopoetic movement of the 1980s, to the current individualist incarnation of MGTOW. This is further reflected in M5, where the discussion of marriage is positioned as the individual belief of the author, as evidenced by the lack of first-person plurals and the use of 'I' at the end of the post.

(6.01) I'm just calling it like I see it. (M5)

Finally, motivational appeals appear in the majority of the MGTOW texts and are realised by directly addressing the reader. As well as such direct addresses, M1 and M2 explicitly seek to create new allies and support existing ones by claiming that the goals of the movement are selfless and encouraging readers to use the MGTOW logo or contact MGTOW. Furthermore, M1 employs a *topos of advantage* of the *pro bono publico* variety. In other words, the manifesto argues that the goals of MGTOW will not just be beneficial for the in-group, but also for 'everyone, including women and children'. Therefore, people should be supportive of MGTOW and seek to fulfil the group's aims of instilling masculinity in others and themselves (see Table 5).

(6.02) Every man supporting this idea is welcome to use the logo in this or similar contexts. (M1)

(6.03) They're [*sic*] are many honest reasons a man will go his own way, just ask one. (M2)

Having established the above features, we first discuss the ideological background of MGTOW via interdiscursive references within the texts and then analyse the representation of the in-group and out-groups in the manifestos.

6.1 Interdiscursivity

Although past literature on the contemporary MGTOW group indicates that they do not view themselves as a movement (Wright et al., 2020), the first manifesto (M1) in the data set exhibits the classic characteristics of political manifestos as established in Section 3, and is also explicitly labelled as a manifesto in the title. Indeed, M1 states the libertarian, even anarchist, goals of the movement and then sets out practical strategies for achieving them:

(6.04) This goal is to take away everyone's 'right' to vote on other people's affairs thus rendering it impossible for political organisms and ideologies to impose their personal will on everyone else. (M1)

M1 also orients itself by referencing the political ideologies of feminism and socialism in its 'prime strategies', in order to disaffiliate the movement from them.

(6.05) It is not about reinstalling patriarchy or revoking female voting rights or making socialism illegal. It might have this as a side effect – but not directly and not as a political ideology (M1)

By noting these potential side effects of MGTOW (example 6.06), the author suggests that the movement is capitalist and right-wing in nature. To an extent, traces of capitalist logic are present in M1 and M4, too, as gender relations are framed in terms of trade and cost vs benefit. However, this economic framing is achieved using metaphor as opposed to explicitly advocating capitalism.

(6.06) Femininity will be the <u>price</u> women <u>pay</u> for enjoying masculinity in men! (M1)

(6.07) a simple <u>cost/benefit</u> analysis of the dating <u>market</u> (M4)

Turning to the later manifestos, a right-wing libertarian stance is established through naming the state as an out-group (discussed in more detail in Section 6.4) which infringes on the freedoms of its citizens:

(6.08) As <u>the centralized state</u> has risen in prominence, we see the decline of families. <u>The state</u> has a direct incentive to raise your children for you, because the state wants to raise mental slaves. (M5)

The author of M5 also explicitly aligns himself with a far-right ideology and combines this with references to mediaeval history and the video game series *Dark Souls*. An interest in European mediaeval history has been associated with the far-right, who utilise narratives and symbols from this era to support white nationalist beliefs (Young, 2021). Gaming culture has also been associated with the alt-right to some extent, although this is certainly not applicable to the subculture as a whole (Marwick & Lewis, 2017).

(6.09) If I had a choice, we'd all be living in a hard right dictatorship, and our cities would look like medieval Europe on steroids (think Lordran from Dark Souls). (M5)

When compared to M1, example 6.09 shows the ideological development of MGTOW from libertarian to authoritarian right in less than 20 years. MGTOW are further aligned with right-wing ideology via disaffiliative intertextual references to mainstream media sources (The Guardian, CNN, Time) and affiliative references to articles by commentator Milo Yiannopoulos from the far-right media outlet Breitbart (M4). Despite these references, it should be noted that in the more recent manifestos, the idea that MGTOW are a political movement is explicitly rejected: through *a topos of definition*, the author of M2 argues that MGTOW are 'more of a philosophy on how to live life instead of a movement'. According to him, MGTOW share neither the structure nor the goals of a political movement, as they are a 'bunch of guys' rather than an 'organized social group operating to achieve a certain goal' and they aim to 'opt out' of the status quo rather than change it. Consequently, MGTOW do not match the definition of a social movement and should not be considered one (see also Section 3).

MGTOW manifestos also utilise an academic register when stating their beliefs. External sources are used to support claims made by the in-group. For example, M2 provides an affiliative link to a 'source' from the now defunct social networking site Experience Project to support the notion that men do not require romantic partners. Furthermore, academic literature from the fields of gender studies and neuropsychiatry is referenced in M3 (see Table 5). This literature is used to support unmodalised statements from the author about innate features of men and women. It is probably no coincidence that the author has chosen to reference two books by female writers, that is, out-group members, to lend further credibility to his claims. This academic tone is boosted by the use of statistics as well as the indefinite article plus singular noun structure to convey a sense of objectivity

(6.10) Surveys show that <u>40 per cent</u> of people in marriages report they are lonely (M3).

(6.11) <u>A man</u> on the other hand, will have a detailed knowledge of all sorts of information that has no practical applications for him. (M3)

References are also made in M4 to concepts from evolutionary psychology (e.g., humans are described as an 'animal species' who 'would willfully abstain from spreading its genes'), which is a feature of manosphere discourse more broadly (see Van Valkenburgh, 2021). This dehumanisation further cements the notion that the actions of men and women are innate and pre-determined by evolution.

Furthermore, M3 uses a *topos of threat* and a *topos of disadvantage* to convince readers not to believe in the myth of the soulmate, because it is 'dangerous' and encourages people to 'waste their time'. These arguments are then supported through a *topos of authority* and *topos of numbers*. The author cites unnamed 'surveys' and 'studies' which supposedly suggest that people who have found a soulmate still experience loneliness and that older people are less lonely. However, no further information is given about the studies, such as titles or authors names. This means that readers cannot verify the quality, or even the existence, of these sources. The author here also refers to his own 'theory' about the relationship between ageing and loneliness, thus presenting himself as a credible source on the subject.

(6.12) <u>Studies</u> show that people actually experience less loneliness as they grow older. (M3)

(6.13) My <u>theory</u> is that older people experience loneliness less because they grow more comfortable with themselves. (M3)

However, this academic tone is not held consistently. M3 contains various spelling mistakes, while M4 contains much taboo language, and the author admits to having merely 'skimmed' the articles from the mainstream media sources.

Having contextualised the MGTOW manifestos in terms of their ideological stance, we now present our findings on how groups of social actors are represented within them.

6.2 Inter-Group Dynamics

We first consider the generalisations made about groups and how an us-vs-them dichotomy is created between them. We will then discuss how the in-group (MGTOW) are represented in the manifestos, followed by a discussion of the various out-groups identified in them.

6.2.1 Generalising about Groups

Broad generalisations are made about men and women as monolithic groups, and both are represented as innately different from one another. In M3, much of this is backed up with academic references, as discussed above, and in one instance, these references are used to support a dehumanising analogy which likens men and women to animals:

(6.14) A <u>tadpole</u> and a <u>frog</u> are from the same species, obviously the brain structure and behaviour of a tadpole differs greatly from a frog. (M3)

Using unmodalised statements, men are represented as knowledgeable (see example 6.11) and women as both inherently social and as ideally having qualities which are perceived as feminine ('nurturing, supporting, and responsible', M1).

Viewing these motherly qualities as superior to others suggests that MGTOW perceive women in terms of what they can provide to men. Somewhat paradoxically, the traits seen as masculine ('self-reliant, proud, and independent', M1) adhere to traditional gender norms by positioning men as confident and able to take care of themselves. Furthermore, traits which exist outside of these norms, in part due to the supposed influence of the feminist movement, are seen as superfluous.

(6.15) By instilling masculinity in men, we make men self-reliant, proud, and independent. By instilling femininity in women, we make them nurturing, supporting, and responsible ... Women having 'other qualities' is not interesting to men because we don't need them! (M1)

The desired feminine traits are also described as 'the price women pay' (see example 6.06), which frames feminine traits as a punishment or a sacrifice rather than something women would choose to embody out of their own free will. Nevertheless, the pattern of definite article plus singular noun in example 6.16 conveys that feminism has been detrimental to all Western women.

(6.16) Feminism has ruined the Western woman. (M4)

Vague quantifiers are also used to make generalisations about both MGTOW and women, which allows for the possibility that these generalisations are not universally applicable. For instance, MGTOW are represented as a pluralistic group who often have financial freedom whereas women are described as initiating divorces 'the majority of the time' (M2).

(6.17) Since a lot of MGTOWS don't have to support a family, a lot of their money turns into disposable income. (M2)

Similarly, the claim that women only have certain types of knowledge is somewhat hedged, using the vague quantifier 'most'. It should be noted though that unmodalised statements about men and women were far more common in the data.

(6.18) To operate an automobile, limited knowledge is required ... This is the knowledge most women have of automobiles. (M3)

The next subsection will show that gendered groups are not only homogenised, but also set in opposition to each other.

6.2.2 Creating an Us-vs-Them Dichotomy

VIOLENCE metaphors were the most common type of metaphor used to create an us-vs-them dichotomy. MGTOW and men more broadly are positioned

against societal expectations of men ('<u>fighting</u> chivalry', M1) and denounce-
ments from out-groups (framed as '<u>attacks</u>' in M2). In M5, marriage is likened
to being shot for no reason and therefore as posing a high risk to the in-group
and as something to be avoided. The fact that these metaphors and similes are
present in both the earlier and later manifestos indicate that conceptualising out-
groups in terms of violent threats is central to MGTOW ideology.

(6.19) Trying to get married today in order to provide a stable household for
raising children is a fool's errand. It's like trying to <u>catch a bullet</u> for your
friend to save his life, but that friend doesn't even like you and the <u>bullet</u>
wasn't going to hit him anyway. (M5)

M5 also uses a *topos of disadvantage*: marriage in contemporary society is
represented as a 'fool's errand' as it will not help men to achieve their goal of
raising their children. Furthermore, the manifesto also states that 'today, nobody
is asking' and 'nobody wants' men to get married. This suggests that there may
have been a time in the past where marriage *was* a requirement and that the only
reason why men would get married is because it was expected of them. Overall,
the manifesto argues that there are no longer any benefits or reasons for
marriage and therefore it should be avoided.

Metaphors pertaining to force and space were also present, with feminists
represented as applying 'pressure' to those they disagree with (M3), and as
'ruin[ing] things on the other <u>side</u> of the <u>aisle</u>, too' (M4), thus constructing
feminism as a negative influence on both men and women. Metaphors of force
are also used to frame men and women as innately different, with behavioural
differences being attributed to uncontrollable neurological factors:

(6.20) These are <u>forces</u> due to the different brain structure and occur on
a subconscious level. (M3)

Adversative conjunctions such as 'instead of', 'on the other hand' and 'while'
are other means of constructing men and women in this way. For instance, the
communication styles of men and women are described as mutually exclusive in
both M1 and M3, and the idea that women act in a supposedly masculine
manner is seen as negative and potentially threatening to the dominant social
position of men:

(6.21) we induce women to take a complementary position with men <u>instead of</u>
a competitive position, as is now the case. (M1)

Furthermore, in M2 both women and men who hold supposed misconceptions
about MGTOW are directly addressed in order to correct this.

(6.22) A lot of women think this is what MGTOW is all about. If this is <u>you</u> too, guess what? <u>You</u>'re wrong. (M2)

Although 'newbies browsing this sub[reddit]' (M2) are identified as the intended audience of M2, the author directly addresses women to assert that they should not expect certain behaviours, both positive and negative, from MGTOW.

(6.23) Don't like being catcalled in the street? No problem, they wont[sic] catcall <u>you</u>. Hate being stared at the gym? Fine by them, they wont[sic] look … What people forget that this is a double edge sword. Having a guy buy <u>you</u> drinks at a bar? Nope! Taking <u>you</u> out to a nice expensive dinner and picking up the tab? Nope! (M2)[9]

By addressing these audiences, the MGTOW authors create clear expectations of in-group behaviour as well as who is or is not part of that in-group.

6.3 In-Group

We now consider how MGTOW represent themselves as positive, as a broadly cohesive group, and as lacking power in wider society due to their identity as men.

6.3.1 Positively Representing the In-Group

MGTOW explicitly evaluate themselves positively in both M1 and M2 for their popularity, well-roundedness, goals and attitudes. As discussed above, M2 is dedicated to defining what it means to be a MGTOW, and so the in-group is defined positively as 'the largest (and coolest) wing of the '"man-o-sphere"' (M2). It should, however, be noted that before the MGTOW subreddit was quarantined, it had comparatively fewer subscribers than the men's rights activists and pick-up artist subreddits (Ribeiro et al., 2020). Zuckerberg (2018, p. 19) also confirms that '[t]he community of Men Going Their Own Way is smaller than the men's human rights movement and seduction communities'. Yet metaphoric expressions such as 'MGTOW is <u>growing</u>' (M2) and the movement's 'spread' (M2), as well as the name MGTOW itself, position them as a thriving, popular and agentive community. MGTOW are also positively evaluated as having fulfilling lives separate from women in terms of having support networks and a good work/life balance:

---

[9] This refusal to meet women's perceived expectations is reminiscent of the artist E. Jane's feminist manifesto declaring to live in 'the land of NOPE' (2016).

(6.24) They have friends, they most definitely have hobbies, they have family, they have good jobs, and they have fun (M2)

Furthermore, in M1, the movement is associated with being supportive of others by 'working for freedom and justice', listing 'support[ing] other men' in its aims and claiming that the goals of the movement are beneficial to women and children as well as men (see Table 5). Thus, earlier MGTOW position their movement as not solely for the benefit of men.

On the other hand, M2 uses the *pro bono nobis* version of the *topos of advantage* in order to emphasise the benefits for the in-group specifically. Men's separatist lives are described using positive, sometimes intensified adjectives ('very content', 'good jobs', 'very peaceful', 'orderly') and nouns ('luxury', 'dreams'). Financial benefits are highlighted, as the manifesto mentions that MGTOW are more likely to have disposable income due to their lack of spending obligations (see example 6.17). Implicitly, this assumes that having a good job, free time and disposable income are mutually exclusive with marriage or family life. Therefore, if men want access to these benefits, they need to go their own way.

This mutual exclusivity between marriage and a happy lifestyle becomes more explicit in the fifth point in the manifesto, where it is argued that marriage means 'giving up all your hobbies, your awesome life style [*sic*] and pursuing your dreams'. A juxtaposition is created between the 'monotony' of marriage and the 'awesome life style' enjoyed by MGTOW. The author thus uses a *topos of freedom* to argue that men should go their own way, because it is the only way that they will be at liberty to pursue their hobbies.

6.3.2 Creating In-Group Cohesion

The primary method for creating in-group cohesion in the MGTOW manifestos is ascribing thoughts, affect, stance and volition to the whole group. One of the ways this is achieved is through the use of an exclusive 'we' to state the goals of the movement.

(6.25) By holding this point of view, <u>we</u> are helping other men and, more importantly, <u>we</u> are helping boys grow up to become men. (M1)

However, this discussion of goals is unique to M1. Instead, M2 positions the group as sharing a 'philosophy' instead of being a movement and discusses how MGTOW think and feel regarding women, relationships and wider society. This indicates that although MGTOW manifestos as a whole represent MGTOW as a broadly cohesive network with set beliefs, the nature of that network has varied over time.

MGTOW are represented as independent and confident in their separatist beliefs. They are portrayed as free-thinking individuals whose actions are not constrained by societal expectations ('they just don't conform to society', M2), and as not requiring intimate relationships with women ('no need for female companionship', 'not afraid of being alone', 'trying to shame a MGTOW into settling down is pointless', all M2). While the use of negation presents their strength of conviction in absolute terms, the latter example also demonstrates a *topos of disadvantage* by arguing that trying to persuade a MGTOW into marriage is 'pointless' and thus not worth doing. MGTOW are also ascribed speech which asserts their willingness to distance themselves from being treated poorly by various out-groups (see Section 6.4 for more details):

(6.26) They've taken a good logical look at dating, marriage, and they [*sic*] way divorce courts treat them. At that point they decided to <u>say</u> 'screw this i'm <u>out'</u>. (M2)

However, the author of M4 argues that despite the separatist nature of MGTOW, men nevertheless desire the company of women. This is done using first-person plural pronouns which include men as a whole as opposed to just MGTOW. This belies an inherent contradiction in MGTOW, as the extent to which these men desire separation from women is ambiguous.

(6.27) Here's the secret about <u>us</u> dudes; most of <u>us</u> really do want the company of women, just as much as they want <u>ours</u>. (M4)

Furthermore, MGTOW are represented as apathetic about issues which do not personally concern them.

(6.28) They're not all anti-feminist they just couldn't care less about women's rights, issues, etc. Now, don't get me wrong some of MGTOWS are anti-feminist. The rest of them could just care less. (M2)

Although the author of M2 argues that some MGTOW have differing attitudes to feminism, discussions of feminism in the MGTOW manifestos are overwhelmingly negative, indicating a broadly anti-feminist stance.

Turning to how MGTOW reference themselves and each other, unsurprisingly, the principal in-group term for self-reference is the name of the community presented in capital letters. Aside from personal pronoun use, the only other reference term used for in-group members was the gendered relational/kinship term 'brother' (M1), although this only occurred once.

6.3.3 Representing the In-group as Powerless

MGTOW are represented as powerless due to the actions of women, feminists and society as a whole (see Section 6.4 for a more detailed discussion of these out-groups). In particular, they are represented as the victims of false rape accusations, as being taken advantage of and as being verbally harassed. MGTOW also note that one of the reasons that men join them is because they 'have been in abusive relationships' (M2). Sometimes, these representations are achieved in an indirect manner using agentless passives; these representations do not name the out-groups responsible, although they can be inferred from the context.

(6.29) Maybe you'll really hit the anti-lottery and get a false rape claim and have your life ruined. (M4)

(6.30) Things such as shaming them, calling them 'man-boys', having white-knights attack them (M2)

These representations are also achieved using relational processes which frame men as a commodity for women to exploit financially, and this exploitation is seen as encouraged by the government. Men are then impersonalised through the simile of the FedEx delivery service and described as 'slaves', further emphasising the extent to which they feel used and dehumanised. It is also worth noting that in example 6.31, this representation of men as disempowered is contrasted with the image of 'a sassy black woman'. This reference draws on racist stereotypes of Black women as overly assertive (see Troutman, 2022) and links notions of Blackness and womanhood with the negatively evaluated out-group of 'the state'.

(6.31) the state has created a system in which women will get impregnated, and then figure out how to get a man to pay for the kid. This is far more efficient than the government trying to produce and fund the slaves itself. It's like the difference between FedEx and UPS: one guarantees your package gets delivered tomorrow morning, the other makes you stand in line for 40 minutes just to be told by a sassy black woman that you filled out the wrong form. (M5)

Furthermore, M5 presents men as being powerless to stop cultural change that goes against their interests. First, the author uses a *topos of lack of advantage* to argue that 'getting married isn't the way' to help men 'save the West' (see example 6.45), and thus there is no practical reason or advantage in getting married, as it will not help them achieve that goal. However, the reason why this strategy will not work may be because the goal itself is unattainable: through a *topos of history*, the author compares contemporary cultural changes to historical changes such as the industrial revolution and American imperialism. According to M5, American imperialism is too dominant to preserve and revitalise Indigenous traditions and cultural practices. By analogy, it would also be 'useless' for Western men to cling to their own traditions. This analogy naturalises settler colonialism as inevitable and compares the decline in conservative values to the genocide of millions of Native Americans. The argument is also contradictory, because Western culture is simultaneously presented as at risk and in need of saving, but also dominant and hegemonic enough to pose a risk to other cultural values.

(6.32) We may be entering a new age of society, similar to the transition between hunter/gatherer cultures and agricultural ones, or between agricultural and industrial. Maybe fighting to save what he had is as useless as trying to save the Native American way of life from Imperial Americanism (M5).

Another central way in which MGTOW construct their in-group identity is by establishing various out-groups to differentiate themselves from; we now discuss these in detail.

6.4 Out-Groups

The primary out-group in the MGTOW manifesto is, unsurprisingly, women, and the named secondary out-groups are men who are not MGTOW, a conceptualisation of big government referred to as 'the state', and mainstream media outlets. There are also unnamed detractors of the MGTOW community who are solely represented through hypothetical ascribed speech. Leaving these groups unnamed potentially serves to present the arguments made on behalf of them as being universal to multiple out-groups. In terms of content, this ascribed speech indicates that out-group members think that MGTOW should stop complaining and should act like adults, and that they favour social constructionism over biological essentialism.

(6.33) People who dislike MGTOW really can't seem to come to terms with this. All the time you the [*sic*] see them <u>telling</u> MGTOWS to 'man up!' or <u>say</u> that they have 'peter pan syndrome'. (M2)

(6.34) Ester Villar's [*sic*] book was <u>criticized</u> because it was <u>argued</u> these things are caused by the social constructs. (M3)

6.4.1 Women

Women are explicitly evaluated as negative by ascribing affect and stances to them which position relationships with them as costly and risky to men. For instance, women are represented as unfaithful and otherwise mistreating men in marriage and relationships. Women are also infantilised by referring to them as relying on men and by describing them (alongside children) as society's 'dependents' (M5).

(6.35) Men stuck paying alimony to a <u>cheating</u> ex wife who divorced him. Men <u>screwed over sideways</u> in family courts for child custody. Then it spread to men in marriages who were downright miserable with the way their wives <u>treated them</u>. Then it spread to men in relationships that were fed up with the dating world and how they <u>were expected</u> to act, despite being <u>taken advantage of</u> by women. (M2)

Women's physical appearance and personalities are also negatively evaluated. Repeatedly in M4, the physical appearance of feminist women is insulted and framed as undesirable to the in-group, particularly when it does not align with normative expressions of femininity:

(6.36) In solidarity with their <u>unfuckable</u> foremothers, they <u>cut their hair short</u>, <u>get fat</u>, and become equally <u>unfuckable</u>, somehow convincing themselves that this is what they 'want'. This flies in the face of what women *really* want – to be protected and nurtured in the company of high-quality men. (M4, original emphasis)

The reference to 'foremothers' in the example above references a previous generation of feminists, thus equating short hair and being overweight with a feminist identity. This generation is also referred to as 'bitter', as being 'past the wall' (i.e., too old to be considered attractive to the in-group) and as verbally expressing hatred towards men. There is some reference to hatred for men in the lesbian separatist data ('separatists live with the added oppression of judgement, ostracism, and ridicule when we are out about <u>hating</u> men', L2), but ascribing that feeling to a whole generation of feminists is obviously a generalisation. That generation is then credited with influencing younger women to act against their supposedly true desires, thus supporting the in-group's negative opinion of feminism.

(6.37) Bitter older women past the wall <u>rant</u> about how men are the enemy who must be hated, creating an anti-male circlejerk. In order to conform to the groupthink, as women so often do, younger women pile on and <u>agree</u> to their man-hating sentiments. (M4)

In the same post, feminist women are dehumanised as 'the <u>product</u> of this cultural <u>virus</u>' (M4). Feminism is thus linked to an infectious disease, which should be avoided by limiting contact with feminists. This is in line with Sobieraj's assertion that 'extraordinary venom is saved for feminists and women who are otherwise noncompliant with gendered expectations, such as those who are overweight and body positive' (2018, p. 10).

Women are described as 'neurotic' and are also repeatedly referred to as 'cunts' in M4, explicitly referencing female genitalia in a derogatory manner and metonymically equating women with their vulvas.

(6.38) Don't surrender your life to a neurotic cunt who doesn't appreciate you. (M4)

In example 6.38, relations between men and women are additionally framed using war terminology. This highlights the seriousness of the threat that women are seen to pose to men.

Furthermore, M2 is dedicated to debunking the views that women supposedly hold about MGTOW. These views are expressed by ascribing speech and thoughts to women via hypothetical formulations, making intertextual references to women discussing MGTOW and discussing what female friends have said to them. For instance, women are represented as calling MGTOW 'isolated' and referring to them in a derogatory manner as 'hermits' and 'bitter men who cant [*sic*] get a date' (M2). In all instances, ascribed speech and thought is brought up in order to be refuted by the in-group.

(6.39) Females seem to think that a MGTOW is some guy living his [*sic*] mom's basement who refuses to leave and live life … Calling them hermits is seriously missing the mark. (M2)

(6.40) In a Youtube video called 'Dear Men' by Alexanda Blue she mention [*sic*] that guys were isolating themselves from society. (M2)

(6.41) When I talked about MGTOW to a female friend, she asked 'Aren't they afraid of being lonely?' (M2)

Relationships with women are generally presented as detrimental to men. For example, the author of M2 uses a *topos of finance*. In addition to losing disposable income, it is argued that a man 'could potentially lose at least half his assets' in the event of a divorce. The pre-modifier 'at least' suggests that men could in fact stand to lose even more than half, meaning the risk is even greater. The use of the possessive pronoun 'his' implies that all of the marital assets such as income and property rightfully belong to the man and that the woman has no legitimate claim to these assets. This argument reinforces the common belief within the manosphere and men's rights communities that divorce courts are biased against men, making men worse off financially after divorce (Kaye & Tolmie, 1998; Lin, 2017).

M4 provides further examples of how men can be victimised in relation-ships with women. First, the author uses a *topos of threat* to argue that men should not date women in order to mitigate the risk of having their 'life ruined' by a 'false rape claim'. Second, a *topos of finance* is used to argue that men could 'lose everything in a divorce'. This is a step up from M2, where it was argued that men could lose 'at least half' of their assets. Finally, the author of M4 argues that there are no advantages to dating women because they are 'fucking cunts' who 'aren't fun to be around'. Overall, relationships pose too many negative consequences for men, and women do not possess any pleasant qualities which could make a relationship worth the risk. Consequently, the author can argue that men ought to go their own way.

It should be noted that women are the only out-group to also be represented in a positive manner, although this is done hypothetically. As discussed in Section 6.2.1, women are described in terms of feminine qualities that the in-group desire:

(6.42) Feminine qualities we want from women: – Nurturing – Supportive – Responsibility – Respectfulness – Honesty (M1)

While it is noteworthy that this representation only occurs in the oldest mani-festo in our data set, Krendel (2020) also finds evidence of hypothetical submissive women being represented positively in the MGTOW subsection of r/TheRedPill. This suggests that this feature is present in both the older and contemporary MGTOW community to some extent.

6.4.2 'The State'

The right-wing libertarian stance of MGTOW is visible through the way the manifestos frame both wider society and the government as out-groups, as both are seen as unduly influencing men's lives. For this reason, M1 states that the aim of MGTOW is 'to be independent of society, and live within it, while at the same time work for limiting governmental influence upon our daily lives' (M1). Specifically, the government is framed as having legal powers and the ability to control immigration, both of which are seen as having an adverse effect on men's lives. In example 6.43, it is argued that the government's supposed support for sexual harassment and rape cases is responsible for men being unwilling to participate in intimate relationships.

(6.43) The majority of men are single yet off-the-market. Especially in a society where a guy [is] one false rape accusation or sexual harassment case away from a jail sentience [*sic*]. (M2)

Furthermore, M5 implicitly references the 'white genocide' far-right conspiracy theory, which argues that non-white populations are slowly replacing white ones, with the government enabling this via their migration policies.

(6.44) the <u>dire</u> situation that our (Western) culture seems to find itself in, namely demographic decline due to feminism and the resultant solution of importing a mass of third world foreigners to make up for our lack of babies (M5)

6.4.3 Men Who Are Not MGTOW

The author of M4 uses the adjective 'beta' to describe men who choose to date women. Within the manosphere, 'beta' is a derogatory term for men that connotes negative traits such as (below) average physical attractiveness, emotional and physical weakness, subordination to women and 'alpha' males, and complicitness in their own exploitation by placing women on pedestals (Ging, 2019; Jones et al., 2020; Preston et al., 2021). Within the manifesto, it is also argued that there are no advantages to dating women: dating is described as a 'loser's game' where 'everyone loses'. If men try to pursue relationships with women, they turn into 'unfuckable beta weenies'. In other words, men become undesirable and physically weak, so will be even *less* likely to succeed in attracting women. Therefore, the best solution is to stop playing the 'game' altogether.

That said, out-group men are not exclusively represented in a derogatory manner. Although marriage is consistently represented as negative in the MGTOW manifestos, some men who marry women are represented as having idealistic reasons for doing so. In M5, these men are ascribed hypothetical speech which represents them as somewhat noble and aligns them with the author's right-wing views:

(6.45) I get that guys <u>want</u> to 'Save the West.' In a sense, I do as well. But getting married isn't the way to do it. (M5)

6.4.4 Mainstream Media

Lastly, as discussed above, mainstream media outlets are evaluated in an explicitly negative manner, with hyperbolic and untrue beliefs and stances being ascribed to them. According to M4, when discussing a study which claimed that millennials are having less sex than past generations, MGTOW position the grounds that mainstream media outlets give for this phenomenon as unreasonable. This includes lifestyle and education factors (e.g., 'they say we're too busy, they say it's because we're living at home, they say we're more aware of the dangers of STDs', M4) along with women's changing attitudes towards casual relationships. These attitudes are positioned as external to the in-group via the reported speech markers 'they say' and 'they even suggest'. These ascribed attitudes are framed as unreasonable via the stance marker 'even' and via hyperbole which dehumanises men and depicts them as violent:

(6.46) they <u>even</u> <u>suggest</u> that women are afraid of 'slut shaming'. (M4)

(6.47) these same sources <u>tell</u> women that men are a bunch of <u>animals</u> who want to savagely beat them and rape them. (M4)

Furthermore, the microblogging and content sharing site Tumblr and individual bloggers are represented negatively as teaching men to compromise their sense of masculinity to attract women. In example 6.48, they are placed in an active position as sayers of the verbal process 'tell', which demonstrates the extent to which the in-group view such platforms as powerful and agentive.

(6.48) Tumblr, the blogosphere, and the MSM [mainstream media] <u>tell</u> men that in order to win a woman's affections, you must become a goony beta weenie with no self respect (M4)

In summary, based on the manifestos analysed in this data set, MGTOW can be described as a right-wing libertarian group with some evidence of far-right authoritarian overlap. However, it cannot necessarily be categorised as a political or social movement: although MGTOW are described as such in M1, later manifestos instead describe them in terms of individual actions and philosophy.

The manifestos are characterised by broad generalisations made about men and women, who are positioned in an adversarial dichotomy. There is only one in-group, MGTOW themselves, who are represented as broadly cohesive (although some minor differences are acknowledged) and are represented as positive but powerless. Although they describe themselves as a popular and distinct section of the wider manosphere, a supportive group and strong in their convictions, they also see themselves as abused and exploited by four different out-groups. There is one primary out-group, women, who are also represented as unattractive and as feminist, as well as three secondary out-groups: men who are not MGTOW, 'the state' and mainstream media outlets. The fact that women are occasionally represented positively (albeit hypothetically) and the in-group is represented as powerless indicates that van Dijk's (1998) ideological square of positive in-group and negative out-group representation does not hold unequivocally true for this data.

Having established the interdiscursivity, discourse functions, language features and arguments of both the lesbian separatist and MGTOW manifestos, we will compare the two in the next section.

7 Comparison and Discussion

In this section, we discuss the similarities and differences between the lesbian separatist and MGTOW manifestos, with regard to their use of interdiscursivity, discourse functions, language features and argumentative *topoi*. We will also consider the extent to which both groups can be viewed as extremist and potentially hateful towards their respective out-groups.

7.1 Similarities

Both types of manifestos homogenise groups of people using vague quantifiers and unmodalised statements. A dichotomy is constructed between these groups using FORCE, SPACE and VIOLENCE metaphors. Broadly cohesive in-groups are established using in-group reference terms, which are sometimes capitalised, an exclusive 'we' and relational or kinship terms. Both in-groups and out-groups are ascribed affect, stance and volition. In broad adherence with van Dijk's (1998) notion of an ideological square, the in-group is presented in a positive manner in both data sets by means of explicit evaluation, whereas out-groups are represented negatively through explicit evaluation, dehumanising metaphors and ascribed speech. There are some instances though where this is not the case (see 7.2). Members of the so-called 'opposite sex' are the primary out-group for both sets of authors and are presented as a threat to the in-group. Their negative effect on the in-group is expressed by presenting the in-group as powerless, by means of agentless passives and relational processes, occasionally in combination with references to violence and abuse. Secondary out-groups are members of the same gender who are not part of the in-group, for example, non-separatist feminists or married men. Although both the in-group and out-groups are addressed, there is one manifesto in each set (L2 and M2) which is solely dedicated to rectifying misconceptions that out-groups have about the in-group and which addresses out-group members directly. This focus on out-groups in both types of manifesto mirrors political manifestos written by opposition parties who are not in power (Pearce, 2014; Szenes, 2021). It is also of note that both types of manifesto draw on political ideologies, albeit very different ones (socialism vs libertarianism and right-wing anarchism or authoritarianism), and that in both sets of manifestos, there is a shift in focus away from collective action and towards individual engagements with the movements and networks, respectively.

Regarding similarities in argumentation strategies, both groups use the *topos of advantage* to present separatism as beneficial: *pro bono nobis* to emphasise the benefits to the in-group (such as a peaceful lifestyle or intellectual creativity) and *pro bono publicum* to argue that separatism is advantageous for society as a whole. Similarly, both lesbian separatists and MGTOW employ the *topos of freedom,* where one of the purported benefits of separatism for the in-group is an increased level of personal freedom and autonomy. For lesbian separatists, freedom means liberation from male dominance, while for MGTOW freedom means the ability to pursue one's hobbies and desired career path without being burdened by a female partner. Furthermore, both groups use the *topos of authority* in order to bolster their claims, although the source of the authority differs (see 7.2).

Turning to similarities in manifesto characteristics (see Holland, 2014), as illustrated above, both data sets focus heavily on allocating roles (i.e., in-groups and out-groups) and establishing ethical norms, the latter via specific lexis, relational processes and negation. Also, both use an academic register in places, and both make use of intertextual references to support the arguments being made, which evokes an authoritative and official tone (Taub & Hamo, 2011; Scarabicchi, 2020). It should be noted though that MGTOW draw mostly on evolutionary psychology and reference 'science' 'studies', 'source[s]' and numbers, while lesbian separatists engage in a nominal writing style (e.g., in L3). Finally, lesbian separatist and MGTOW manifestos alike relate folklore narratives, albeit in different ways (see 7.2), and issue motivational appeals to persuade others to join them.

7.2 Differences

Starting with the manifesto characteristics, we can see that these are realised differently in the two data sets. Firstly, considering folklore narratives, one lesbian separatist manifesto (L1) relays its mythological origins through a narrative introduction, perhaps following the example of the influential manifesto *The Woman Identified Woman* (Radicalesbians, 1970), while two MGTOW authors (M3 and M4) use intertextual references to evoke culturally salient texts. The ways in which ethical norms are realised differ as well: where the authors of L1 use deontic modality to put women under obligation (see Table 4), the writer in M2 instead employs vague quantifiers ('Alot [*sic*] of MGTOW's avoid women all together'), thereby enacting a version of the *topos of people* (Reisigl, 2014, p. 78). Furthermore, as part of a fully fledged social movement, the lesbian separatist authors set more store by strategic planning, using additional dynamic and deontic modality as well as cause-effect and temporal conjunctions (see Table 4; also 'we <u>need</u> absolutely safe, female-only space', L5; '<u>In order to</u> get out from under male domination', L3). Lastly, utopian schemes are posited in the early manifestos for MGTOW, but not in the later ones, which potentially indicates a dwindling sense of optimism for the network.

When it comes to generalising about gendered groups, the MGTOW manifestos show no absolute quantifiers. We could read this as a reaction to anticipated or experienced criticism; rather than engaging with it in a question-and-answer format as the author of L2 does, the MGTOW writers may prefer to hedge their claims. However, there are absolute quantifiers in other manosphere data sets (see Aiston, 2023; Krendel et al., 2022). Their use of numbers (example 6.10) and analogies from zoology (example 6.14) further seeks to lend credibility to their argument. The male separatist authors also use phrases combining articles with singular nouns (example 6.16), but it should be noted that the Radicalesbians' seminal manifesto *The Woman Identified Woman* (1970) features the same construction ('<u>A lesbian</u> is the rage of all women condensed to the point of explosion. She is <u>the woman</u> who . . .'). In terms of constructing a dichotomy between men and women, only MGTOW manifestos feature adversatives to do so (e.g., 'Women are more concerned about social connections <u>while</u> men are more concerned about facts', M3). In fact, the lesbian separatist manifestos do not show direct comparisons of men and women at all, suggesting that their lesbian authors are not as interested in how women and men differ or relate to each other.

The two data sets are very similar when it comes to constructing the in-group, the main difference being that only lesbian separatists use a BUILDING metaphor to create in-group cohesion. L1, for instance, refers to 'build[ing] a movement' and L3 to 'building lesbian culture'. By contrast, male separatists reject calling themselves a social movement at all (Wright et al., 2020) and indeed, the leftist history of the concept would be at odds with the right-wing anarchist and libertarian ideologies that characterise MGTOW discourse.

We can note more secondary out-groups for the MGTOW manifestos, as their authors set themselves apart not only from non-MGTOW men but also from more abstract entities such as 'the state' and mainstream media. This demarcation illustrates their overlap with right-wing beliefs even more clearly than their rejection of the social movement label (Panizo-Lledot et al., 2019). When negatively evaluating the various out-groups, lesbian separatists alone use RELIGION metaphors and hyperbole to do so. Religious terms such as 'cult', 'genuflect' and 'proselytize' (all L5) are harnessed for negative out-group evaluation, while hyperbolic formulations refer to the impossibility of being truly separate from powerful majority out-groups and express the writers' subsequent frustration (e.g., 'Most separatists ... have to deal *daily*, *constantly* with men', L2, original emphasis). Interestingly, only the mostly heterosexual MGTOW writers engage in positive, if hypothetical, out-group representation. Their notion of the ideal woman is part of their alternative universe.

Although both groups use the *topos of authority,* there are notable differences in how this *topos* is realised. MGTOW manifestos tend to employ the *topos of external authority* and the *topos of numbers* in order to support their arguments through the expertise of others, such as citations of academic texts or reporting the results of surveys. This may function to present themselves as credible, intelligent and rational. On the other hand, lesbians are more likely to use a *topos of internal authority* and present themselves as credible authority figures in their own right due to their identities and lived experiences as lesbians and feminist activists. However, the most recent lesbian separatist manifesto does cite external sources. This could be due to the affordances of the digital medium, as the author is able to insert hyperlinks to other blogs and articles, whereas this would not be possible for the earlier texts.

Furthermore, there are differences in the frequency of certain *topoi*. Lesbian separatist manifestos use the *topos of history* more frequently than MGTOW to refer to lessons learnt from previous social movements, such as feeling alien- ated from both women's and gay liberation movements or collaborating with the AIDS movement. This could be because lesbian separatists have a much longer history than MGTOW: while the first MGTOW manifesto was published in 2001, the network only rose to prominence during the late 2010s (Ribeiro et al., 2020). Lesbian separatists also use the *topos of definition* more frequently than MGTOW, in order to argue who can and who cannot be part of a group and what traits can be expected from someone belonging to that group. Third, lesbian separatists are more likely to use the *topos of humanitarianism,* which may speak to socialist influences on lesbian separatism and their discussions of intersectionality and other forms of oppression, and contrasts sharply with the explicit racism found in some MGTOW writings (see examples 6.31, 6.44).

MGTOW manifestos emphasise the futility and uselessness of heterosexual relationships, particularly marriage. Previous research has described MGTOW as the 'abandon wing' of the manosphere (Lin, 2017, p. 86) and found that MGTOW employ very few calls to action (Wright et al., 2020). Thus, it is perhaps not surprising to see claims that men should avoid taking a perceived pointless action, as opposed to finding an alternative useful action or making changes so that the action would no longer be pointless. Finally, the *topos of finance* is often used within MGTOW manifestos but never within the lesbian separatist manifestos. Clearly, MGTOW identity is strongly linked to economic independence and prioritising profit maximisation. In contrast, some lesbian separatist manifestos highlight the authors' low socio-economic status or downward mobility.

7.3 Discussion

Both lesbian separatism and MGTOW can be regarded as a minority movement or network within the wider context of second-wave feminism and the anti-feminist manosphere, respectively – but can either form of gender-based separatism be called extremist? It is certainly true that both espouse extreme gender-based ideologies in that they go further than most in their norms, goals and strategies. Our analyses show how linguistic and discursive features can lead to a distorted or at least exclusive focus on particular aspects of social reality. However, being extreme is not the same as being extremist: where the former means engaging in black-and-white thinking and holding fringe beliefs, the latter condones violence, even terrorism. To the best of our knowledge, only one lesbian separatist manifesto has ever called for violence against men, namely Valerie Solanas' SCUM manifesto (1967). The acronym stands for an imaginary Society for Cutting up Men, and the manifesto opens by stating:

> This society being, at best, an utter bore and no aspect of society being at all relevant to women, there remains to civic-minded, responsible, thrill-seeking females only to overthrow the government, eliminate the money system, institute complete automation and eliminate the male sex. (p. 215)

Later on, its author says that 'SCUM'll kill all men' (p. 240) with a few exceptions and that 'if SCUM ever strikes, it'll be in the dark with a six inch blade' (p. 243). A year after writing the manifesto, Solanas shot the artist Andy Warhol and the art critic Mario Amaya. Other references to violence seem to have been performative or parodic rather than serious, such as one separatist writer adopting the pseudonym killa-man (1974 [1988]) or Diane DiMassa's (1999) cartoon series *Hothead Paisan: Homicidal lesbian terrorist*.

As a network, MGTOW are likewise not known for calls to, or acts of, violence. A notable exception is the case of Christopher Hasson, a US Coast Guard officer who was imprisoned for unlawful possession of firearms and controlled substances and suspected of plotting domestic terrorism. During the prosecution, it was revealed that r/MGTOW was his most frequently visited website, alongside neo-Nazi and fascist websites, and that he also sought information about incels (Owen, 2020). The r/MGTOW subreddit was quarantined the day after this news was published, leading some journalists to speculate the two events might be connected (Pedroja, 2021). There is also empirical research that has examined the prevalence of extreme language within MGTOW communities. In their computational study relying on a bag-of-words approach, Farrell et al. (2019) found that r/MGTOW produced the highest number of posts expressing misogyny and physical or sexual violence relative to other manosphere-affiliated subreddits in their study. Furthermore, they found that 1.2 per cent of posts on r/MGTOW used 'sexually violent language' (e.g., 'rape', 'sodomise', 'gangbang'), 17.95 per cent used 'physically violent language' (e. g. 'hit', 'punch', 'choke') and 27.9 per cent used 'hostile language' (e.g., 'bitch', 'cunt', 'whore'). In a manual study of tweets by prominent MGTOW Twitter accounts, Jones et al. (2020, pp. 1909–12) calculated that 29 per cent of tweets could be classified as harassing, of which 7 per cent suggested 'violent control' of women, but only 4 per cent were directed at a specific target. While most tweets did not target individual users, they argue that this 'passive' harassment can still cause harm as it is less likely to be condemned as dangerous, allowing MGTOW to produce more of this content. These results suggest a certain level of hateful or hostile language, but promotion of physical violence towards a specific target is infrequent.

As we have seen, explicit expression of hatred as an emotion towards an out-group is rare in the lesbian separatist manifestos and non-existent in their MGTOW counterparts. This has also been noted in past studies of hate against women (Kimmel, 2013; Manne, 2018), which observed that emotions such as fear, anger and entitlement to women's bodies and certain behaviours from women were expressed instead. Furthermore, as discussed in Krendel (2021) with regard to the manosphere, it is important to recognise that hate speech can be defined in multiple ways. There is hate speech which directly targets members of a marginalised out-group and that which evokes negative feelings about a particular out-group without a member of the out-group being present.

In this context, it is helpful to draw on the notion of 'soft hate speech' (Baider et al., 2017, p. 4, original emphasis):

> On the one hand, there is what could be called *hard* hate speech, which comprises prosecutable forms that are prohibited by law, and on the other, there is *soft* hate speech, which is lawful but raises serious concerns in terms of intolerance and discrimination.

Soft speech may 'have a devastating effect on the fabric of social order' (ibid.) as it strengthens pre-existing negative attitudes while challenging and potentially revising positive or neutral attitudes. In doing so, soft hate speech is realised to gather followers to a movement or network.

In sum, the manifestos are similar in constructing homogenous groups and dichotomies between in-groups and out-groups, although there are some differences in how this is linguistically realised and who is classified as secondary out-groups. Also, the lesbian separatist authors realise a more fully fledged ideological square in their evaluation of the in-group versus primary and secondary out-groups. Regarding manifesto characteristics, both groups are similar in focusing on role allocation and establishing ethical norms, but strategic planning and utopian schemes are more prominent among lesbian separatists. Finally, there are some *topoi* common to both groups (e.g., *topos of advantage, authority, freedom*) and some that are preferred by either lesbian separatists (e.g., *topos of definition, history, humanitarianism*) or MGTOW (*topos of finance*).

In the final section, we will conclude by pointing out the contributions our study has made and sketching areas for future research.

8 Conclusion

In this Element, we have established similarities and differences in the language used by two gender-based separatist groups, lesbian separatists and MGTOW. In doing so, we have empirically examined Futrelle's (n.d.) assertion that the MGTOW network is 'a lot like lesbian separatism, but for straight dudes'. Our research shows that there are similarities, but the two are not simply the same phenomenon in reverse. Our comparative analysis contributes to the literature on lesbian discourses, which are under-researched compared to those of other LGBTQ+ identities. Furthermore, we have shed some light on a facet of the manosphere which has hitherto not received as much attention as others (e.g., involuntary celibates). In doing so, we have demonstrated how gender-based separatist discourses can impact on gender relations and laid bare the roots of current debates on toxic masculinity and (trans) women's rights. We also hope that the methods demonstrated in this Element can be applied in other comparative studies of gender-based communities and of the discursive construction of collective identities more broadly. This study is located in the discipline of linguistics, but we hope that the findings will also be of interest to sociologists and historians. Following from this research, there are several promising directions for future research into gender-based separatism.

Although lesbian separatism as a social movement may be largely historical, this does not mean that female separatism is no longer practiced. Intriguingly, MGTOW and their 'red-pill philosophy' have found an equivalent in 'pink pill feminism'. Dispersed over various social media platforms, pink pill feminists seek to show the "true nature" of men, develop a "female dating strategy" and, for some, engage in "reverse sexism". There is also a female separatist community on Reddit, even though the subreddit is relatively small with just 952 members. Furthermore, there are emerging female separatist movements in

Asia. In South Korea, a new feminist movement known as 4B advocates 'Four Nos': no heterosexual sex, relationships, marriage, or child-rearing. The movement was 'conceived as a direct challenge to the patriarchal state and reproductive futurism' (Lee & Jeong, 2021, p. 637), where in response to low fertility rates and an ageing population, the South Korean government enacted policies and strategies to incentivise early marriage and childbirth among young women, such as housing schemes for the newly married. Although there is no official data on the size of the movement, members claim that over 4,000 women follow the 'four nos' (France-Presse, 2019). Furthermore, the 6B4T movement in China expands on the tenets of 4B by advocating that women refuse to buy 'misogynistic products' and begin supporting single women, in addition to rejecting religion, feminine beauty standards, obsessive fan culture of celebrities and idols, as well as Japanese manga and anime, due to the latter's sexist depictions of women (Li, 2021). Clearly, female separatist movements in non-Western contexts are a promising area of future research.

It is also interesting to note that the phenomenon of men eschewing relationships with women is not limited to Western contexts. In Japan, so-called 'herbivore men' choose to not actively pursue relationships with women (Fukasawa, 2007; cited in Morioka, 2013). Although this superficially resembles MGTOW, 'herbivore men' are not anti-feminist but instead orient themselves away from a masculine gender role characterised by sexual confidence and aggression. Indeed, Morioka (2013, p. 2) foregrounds the kind and gentle nature of herbivore men and notes that the 'herbivore' in 'herbivore men' 'can be seen as having the connotation of a man who does not hunt women like a "carnivore" and is thus "safe" from a woman's perspective'. Those who are in relationships with women tend to pursue them slowly and aim for clear communication (Morioka, 2013). To an extent, the phrase 'herbivore men' mirrors the pejorative term 'soy boy', popularised by the far-right, which refers to men lacking traditionally masculine characteristics. We believe that this phenomenon, which shares some characteristics with MGTOW but also reconceptualises what it means to be a Japanese man, is another interesting direction for future research.

Although debates about women's spaces and trans women date back to the early 1970s, the most recent lesbian separatist manifesto we analysed (L5) is notable for its rejection of trans rights and indeed the very existence of trans women as women. This gives rise to the question whether lesbian separatism may overlap with or even have been subsumed under so-called gender-critical feminism. According to Pearce et al. (2020, p. 681), the phrase 'gender critical' 'denotes, less a critical approach to gender, and more an emphasis on claiming "biologically defined" notions of femaleness and womanhood over gender identity and social concepts of gender'. Another phrase, 'gender ideology', suggests an overlap between trans-exclusionary feminist and right-wing, anti-feminist Christians, as does the term 'cult' as a derogatory reference to trans activism (Pearce et al., 2020, pp. 681–2, 685; see also example 5.47). In light of this, the acronym 'TERF' (trans-exclusionary radical feminist) is at least a partial misnomer. As Mackay (2021, p. 52) notes

> Radical Feminism has almost become synonymous with transphobia. . . .
> Nuances such as the differences between political lesbianism, cultural fem-
> inism and separatism . . . do not flow easily or untrammelled into the so-called
> gender debates in the mainstream.

What is forgotten in such debates is that radical feminism is anti-essentialist, believing gender differences to be socially constructed in order to maintain patriarchy. As such, individual women and collectives took both trans-inclusive or -exclusive positions. Radical feminism is linked to lesbian separatism in that radical feminists were involved in building women-only spaces; however, 'living a separatist life was not a hallmark or necessity of Radical Feminist theory' (Mackay, 2021, p. 71). Although the author of L5 identifies as a radical feminist, the essentialism that can be seen in her and some other lesbian separatist writings, along with the reduction of patriarchal society to biologic-ally defined males, is a reflection of cultural rather than radical feminism. To the extent that lesbian separatism is becoming subsumed under gender-critical, trans-exclusionary feminism, such radicalisation calls for further research.

   Overall, we have shown how two gender-based separatist discourses reflect the changing and complex feminist and anti-feminist ideologies of their times. We have further outlined the historical and political background of those discourses and indicated how they are influencing contemporary developments in gender relations. It is our hope that this comparative study inspires further linguistic research on social movements and networks and their manifestos, in order to trace radical and potentially destructive social developments.

References

Aiston, J. (2023). *Argumentation strategies in an online male separatist community*. PhD thesis, Lancaster University.

Aman, I. (2009). Discourse and striving for power: An analysis of Barisan Nasional's 2004 Malaysian general election manifesto. *Discourse & Society*, *20*(6), 659–84.

Archibald, S. (2021). On wimmin's land. *Places*, February. https://doi.org/10.22269/210216.

Baider, F. H., Assimakopoulos, S., & Millar, S. L. (2017). Hate speech in the EU and the C.O.N.T.A.C.T project. In S. Assimakopoulos, F. H. Baider, & S. Millar (eds.), *Online hate speech in the European Union: A discourse analytic perspective* (pp. 1–16). Springer.

Bartley, L. (2019). For the many, not the few: A transitivity analysis of Labour's 2017 manifesto as a driving force for promoting a populist Britain. In E. Hidalgo-Tenorio, M.-A. Benítez-Castro & F. De Cesare (eds.), *Populist discourse: Critical approaches to contemporary politics* (pp.136–51). Routledge.

Bates, L. (2020). *Men who hate women: From incels to pickup artists, the truth about extreme misogyny and how it affects us all*. Simon & Schuster.

Beckerman, J. (2021). To B, or not to b? Why capitalize the 'B' in Black? *NorthJersey.com*, 13 October. Retrieved 5 August 2022, from https://eu.northjersey.com/story/opinion/columnists/2021/10/13/why-capitalize-b-black/5980347001/.

Benford, R. D., & Snow. D. A. (2000). Framing processes and social movements: An overview. *Annual Review of Sociology*, *26*, 611–39. https://www.jstor.org/stable/223459.

Bennett, W. L., & Segerberg, A. (2012). The logic of connective action: Digital media and the personalization of contentious politics. *Information, Communication, & Society*, *15*(5), 739–68. https://doi.org/10.1080/1369118X.2012.670661.

Bly, R. (1990). *Iron John*. Addison-Wesley.

Boss Hunting. (29 October 2019). Men going their own way movement is bitterly jaded but potentially valid. *Boss Hunting*. Retrieved 5 August 2022, from www.bosshunting.com.au/life-style/men-going-their-own-way-movement/.

Brewer, K. B. (1995). Issues of separatism in the work communities of women. *Proceedings of the International Association for Business and Society*, *6*, 25–36. https://doi.org/10.5840/iabsproc199563.

British Association for Applied Linguistics. (2021). *Recommendations on Good Practice in Applied Linguistics.* www.baal.org.uk/wp-content/uploads/2021/03/BAAL-Good-Practice-Guidelines-2021.pdf.

Cadalen, P.-Y. (2020). Republican populism and Marxist populism: Perspectives from Ecuador and Bolivia. In M. Kranert (ed.), *Discursive approaches to populism across disciplines: The return of populists and the people* (pp. 313–37). Palgrave Macmillan.

Carmen. (2015). Rebel girls: On building a better separatism. *Autostraddle,* 30 September. www.autostraddle.com/rebel-girls-on-building-a-better-separatism-309366/.

Clatterbaugh, K. (2000). Literature of the US men's movements. *Signs, 25*(3), 883–94. https://doi.org/10.1086/495485.

Cohen, D. S. (2011). The stubborn persistence of sex segregation. *Colombia Journal of Gender and Law, 20*(1), 51–140. https://doi.org/10.7916/cjgl.v20i1.2618.

Colman, F. (2010). Notes on the feminist manifesto: The strategic use of hope. *Journal for Cultural Research, 14*(4), 375–92. https://doi.org/10.1080/14797581003765333.

Combahee River Collective (1977). The Combahee River Collective statement. In B. Fahs (ed.), *Burn it down! Feminist manifestos for the revolution* (pp. 271–80). Verso.

Coston, B. M., & Kimmel, M. (2013). White men as the new victims: Reverse discrimination cases and the men's rights movement. *Nevada Law Journal, 13,* 368–85. https://scholars.law.unlv.edu/nlj/vol13/iss2/5.

Cox, R. W. (1993). Gramsci, hegemony and international relations. In S. Gill (ed.) *Gramsci, historical materialism and international relations* (pp. 49–66). Cambridge University Press.

Danio, M. (1992). The concept of social movement. *The Sociological Review, 40*(1), 1–25. https://doi.org/10.1111%2Fj.1467-954X.1992.tb02943.x.

Dayter, D., & Rüdiger, S. (2022). *The language of pick-up artists: Online discourses of the seduction industry.* Routledge.

della Porta, D., & Diani, M. (2020). *Social movements: An introduction* (3rd ed.). John Wiley & Sons.

DiMassa, D. (1999). *The complete Hothead Paisan: Homicidal lesbian terrorist.* Cleis Press.

Dixon, J. (1988). Separatism: A look back at anger. In B. Cant & S. Hemmings (eds.) *Radical records: Thirty years of lesbian and gay history* (pp. 42–52). Routledge.

Doyle, G. (1996). No man's land: Lesbian separatism revisited. In N. Godwin, B. Hollows & S. Nye (eds.) *Assaults on convention: Essays on lesbian transgressors* (pp. 178–97). Cassell.

Enszer, J. R. (2014). Rethinking lesbian separatism as a vibrant political theory and feminist practice. Paper presented at the conference *A revolutionary moment: Women's Liberation in the late 1960s and early 1970s*. Boston University, 27–29 March. www.bu.edu/wgs/files/2013/10/Enszer-Rethinking-Lesbian-Separatism.pdf.

Enszer, J. R. (2017). Lesbian books are no longer just for lesbians: Legacies of lesbian print culture. *Journal of Media & Cultural Studies*, *32*(1), 62–72. https://doi.org/10.1080/10304312.2018.1404676.

Fahs, B. (2020). *Burn it down! Feminist manifestos for the revolution*. Verso.

Fairclough, N. (2010). *Critical discourse analysis*. (2nd ed.) Longman.

Farrell, T., Fernandez, M., Novotny, J., & Harith, A. (2019). Exploring misogyny across the manosphere in Reddit. *WebSci '19 Proceedings of the 10th ACM Conference on Web Science*, 87–96. https://doi.org/10.1145/3292522.3326045.

Farrell, W. (1993). *The myth of male power: Why men are the disposable sex*. Simon & Schuster.

Farrukh, F., & Masroor, F. (2021). Portrayal of power in manifestos: Investigating authority legitimation strategies of Pakistan's political parties. *Journal of Language and Politics*, *20*(3), 451–73. https://doi.org/10.1075/jlp.18009.far.

Fox, J. (2004). How men's movement participants view each other. *The Journal of Men's Studies*, *12*(2), 103–18. https://doi.org/10.3149%2Fjms.1202.103.

France-Presse. (17 December 2019). 4B is the feminist movement persuading South Korean women to turn their backs on sex, marriage and children. *South China Morning Post*. Retrieved 5 August 2022, from www.scmp.com/news/asia/east-asia/article/3041058/why-south-korean-women-are-turning-their-backs-sex-marriage-and.

Friedan, B. (1963). *The feminine mystique*. W. W. Norton.

Frye, M. (1978). Some reflections on separatism and power. *Sinister Wisdom*, *6*, 30–9.

Fukasawa, M. (2007). *Boys' encyclopaedia: Respect boys and sober boys*. Nikkei BP. 平成男子図鑑 リスペクト男子と しらふ男子』日経BP社

Futrelle, D. (n.d.). WTF is a MGTOW? A Glossary. *We Hunted the Mammoth*. Retrieved 17 March 2023, from www.wehuntedthemammoth.com/wtf-is-a-mgtow-a-glossary/.

Geraldine, T. (1988). Practising separatism. *Lesbian Ethics*, *3*(2), 3–5.

Get the L out. (n.d.). *About us*. Retrieved 17 March 2023, from www.getthelouotuk.com/index.html.

Gillman, C. P. (1915 [1979]). *Herland*. Pantheon.

Ging, D. (2019). Alphas, betas, and incels: Theorizing the masculinities of the manosphere. *Men and Masculinities*, *22*(4), 638–57. https://doi.org/10.1177%2F1097184X17706401.

Gush, C. (2015). Casting spells for a female future with 70s lesbian separatist Liza Cowan. *Dyke A Quarterly*. Retrieved 1 February 2022, from www .dykeaquarterly.com/2015/12/in-recent-weeks-perhaps-thevery-first-truly-insta-famous-feminist-fashion-item-has-emerged-a-sweatshirt-worn-by-annie-c.html.

Healey, E. (1996). *Lesbian sex wars*. Virago.

Heritage, F., & Koller, V. (2020). Incels, in-groups and ideologies: The representation of gendered social actors in a sexuality-based online community. *Journal of Language and Sexuality*, *9*(2), 152–78. https://doi.org/10.1075/ jls.19014.her.

Hermansson, P., Lawrence, D., Mulhall, J., & Murdoch, S. (2020). *The international alt-right: Fascism for the 21st century?* Routledge.

Hess, J., Langford, J., & Ross, K. (1980). Comparative separatism. In S. L. Hoagland & J. Penelope (eds.) *For lesbians only: A separatist anthology* (pp. 125–31). Onlywomen Press.

Hoagland, S. L. (1987). Lesbian separatism: An empowering reality. *Gossip: A journal of lesbian feminist ethics*, *6*, 24–36.

Hoagland, S. L., & Penelope, J. (1988). *For lesbians only: A separatist anthology*. Onlywomen Press.

Holland, J. (2014). Narrative fidelity to the little red book in the framing efforts of the Red Guard Movement: A theoretical model for foundational documents. *Discourse & Society*, *25*(3), 383–401. https://doi.org/10.1177% 2F0957926513519535.

Holland, J., & Nichele, E. (2016). An ideological content analysis of corporate manifestos: A foundational document approach. *Semiotica*, *208*(1), 79–101. https://doi.org/10.1515/sem-2015-0115.

hooks, b. (2005). The significance of feminism. In S. P. Hier (ed.), *Contemporary sociological thought: Themes and theories* (pp. 233–42). Canadian Scholars' Press.

Jane, E. (2016). Nope (a manifesto). In B. Fahs (ed.) *Burn it down! Feminist manifestos for the revolution* (p. 263). Verso. https://e-janestudio.tumblr .com/post/132335744305/i-am-not-an-identity-artist-just-because-i-am-a.

Jeffreys, S. (1990). *Anticlimax: A feminist perspective on the sexual revolution*. Women's Press.

Jo, B., Strega, L., & Ruston (2015). Introduction to dykes-loving-dykes: Dyke separatist politics, 25 years update. *Bev Jo Radical Lesbian Feminist Writing*. Retrieved 5 August 2022, from https://bevjoradicallesbian.wordpress.com/ 2017/09/10/introduction-to-dykes-loving-dykes-dyke-separatist-politics-25-years-update/.

Johnston, H. (2023). What's in frame, what's in a name? *Discourse Studies*, 25 (2), 259–72.

Johnston, J. (1973). *Lesbian nation The feminist solution*. Touchstone.

Johnston, J. (2006). Was lesbian separatism inevitable? *The Gay & Lesbian Review Worldwide, 26*(1). [online article]. https://glreview.org/article/article-121/.

Jones, C., Trott, V., & Wright, S. (2020). Sluts and soyboys: MGTOW and the production of misogynistic online harassment. *New Media & Society, 22*(10), 1903–21. https://doi.org/10.1177%2F1461444819887141.

Kamra, L., & Sen, D. (2021). Women's collectives and social transformations in South Asia: Negotiations, navigations and self-making. *Journal of South Asian Development, 15*(3), 309–15. https://doi.org/10.1177/0973174120987091.

Karpenko-Seccombe, T. (2021). Separatism: A cross-linguistic corpus-assisted study of word-meaning development in a time of conflict. *Corpora, 16*(3), 379–416. https://doi.org/10.3366/cor.2021.0228.

Kaye, M., & Tolmie, J. (1998). Discoursing dads: The rhetorical devices of fathers' rights groups. *Melbourne University Law Review, 22*, 162–94.

Kelly, A. (2020). *Fear, hate and countersubversion: American antifeminism online*. PhD Thesis, University of East Anglia.

killa-man of the C.L.I.T. Collective (1974). Trying hard to forfeit all I've known. Reprinted in S. L. Hoagland & J. Penelope (eds.), *For lesbians only: A separatist anthology* (pp. 403–7). Onlywomen Press.

Kimbrell, A. (1997). *The masculine mystique*. Random House.

Kimmel, M. (2013). *Angry white men: American masculinity at the end of an era*. Nation Books.

Kimmel, M., & Kaufman, M. (1994). Weekend warriors: The new men's movement. In H. Brod & M. Kaufman (eds.), *Theorizing masculinities* (pp. 259–88). SAGE.

Koller, V. (2008). *Lesbian discourses: Images of a community*. Routledge.

Koller, V. (2010). Lesbian Nation: A case of multiple interdiscursivity. In R. de Cillia, H. Gruber, M. Krzyżanowski & F. Menz (eds.), *Discourse, Politics, Identity* (pp. 369–81). Stauffenburg.

Koller, V. (2012). How to analyse collective identity in discourse: Textual and contextual parameters. *Critical Approaches to Discourse Analysis Across Disciplines, 5*(2), 19–38. www.lancaster.ac.uk/fass/journals/cadaad/wp-con tent/uploads/2015/01/Volume-5_Koller.pdf.

Koller, V. (2014a). Cognitive linguistics and ideology. In J. Littlemore & J. R. Taylor (eds.), *The Bloomsbury companion to cognitive linguistics* (pp. 234–52). Bloomsbury.

Koller, V. (2014b). Applying social cognition research to critical discourse studies: The case of collective identities. In C. Hart & P. Cap (eds.), *Contemporary critical discourse studies* (pp. 147–65). Bloomsbury.

Krendel, A. (2020). The men and women, guys and girls of the 'manosphere': A corpus-assisted discourse approach. *Discourse & Society*, *31*(6), 607–30.

Krendel, A. (2021). From sexism to misogyny: Can online echo chambers stay quarantined? In I. Zempi & J. Smith (eds.), *Misogyny as hate crime* (pp. 99–118). Routledge.

Krendel, A., McGlashan, M., & Koller, V. (2022). The representation of gendered social actors across five manosphere communities on Reddit. *Corpora*, *17*(2), 291–321.

Kupper, J., & Meloy, J. R. (2021). TRAP-18 indicators validated through the forensic linguistic analysis of targeted violence manifestos. *Journal of Threat Assessment and Management*, *8*(4), 174–99. https://doi.org/10.1037/tam0000165.

Lamoureux, M. (24 September 2015). This group of straight men is swearing off women. *Vice*. Retrieved 5 August 2022, from www.vice.com/en_us/article/7bdwyx/inside-the-global-collective-of-straight-male-separatists.

Larman, R. (8 July 2019). Interview with Sage women's space. https://wyqs.co.uk/stories/ideas-about-feminism-and-lesbian-separatism/full-interview/.

Lee, J., & Jeong, E. (2021). The 4B movement: Envisioning a feminist future with/in a non-reproductive future in Korea. *Journal of Gender Studies*, *30*(5), 633–44. https://doi.org/10.1080/09589236.2021.1929097.

Leeds Revolutionary Feminists (1979). Political lesbianism: The case against heterosexuality. Paper presented at the Revolutionary/Radical Feminist conference, Leeds, September; reprinted in *Wires*, *81*, 25–8.

Lettice (1987). Separatism. *Gossip: A journal of lesbian feminist ethics*, *6*, 107–10.

Levy, A. (2009): Lesbian nation: When gay women took to the road. *The New Yorker*, 22 February. www.newyorker.com/magazine/2009/03/02/lesbian-nation.

Li, J. (14 April 2021). A Chinese platform is erasing 'radical' accounts that shun men and the patriarchy. *Quartz*. Retrieved 5 August 2022, from https://qz.com/1996143/chinas-douban-censors-ideas-from-south-korean-feminist-movement/.

Lin, J. L. (2017). Antifeminism online: MGTOW (Men Going Their Own Way). In U. U. Frömming, S. Köhn, S. Fox & M. Terry (eds.), *Digital environments: Ethnographic perspectives across global online and offline spaces* (pp. 77–96). Transcript.

MacDonald, J. (2015). Maybe what feminism needs is separatism, not inclusion. *Feminist Current*, 30 November. www.feministcurrent.com/2015/11/30/18995/.

Mackay, F. (2021). *Female masculinities and the gender wars: The politics of sex*. I. B. Tauris.

Manne, K. (2018). *Down girl: The logic of misogyny*. Oxford University Press.

Martin, J., & White, P. (2005). *The language of evaluation: Appraisal in English*. Palgrave Macmillan.

Marwick, A., & Lewis, R. (2017). *Media manipulation and disinformation online*. Retrieved 5 August 2022, from https://datasociety.net/pubs/oh/DataAndSociety_MediaManipulationAndDisinformationOnline.pdf.

Massanari, A. L. (2018). Rethinking research ethics, power, and the risk of visibility in the era of the 'alt-right' gaze. *Social Media + Society, 4*(2), 1–9. https://doi.org/10.1177%2F2056305118768302.

McAfee, N., & Howard, K. B. (2018). Feminist political philosophy. In E. N. Zalta (ed.), *Stanford encyclopedia of philosophy*. Metaphysics Research Lab, Stanford University. https://plato.stanford.edu/entries/feminism-political/#RadFem.

McGlashan, M., & Krendel, A. (forthcoming, 2023). Keywords of the manosphere. *International Journal of Corpus Linguistics*.

Messner, M. A. (1998). The limits of 'the male sex role' an analysis of the men's liberation and men's rights movements discourse. *Gender and Society, 12*(3), 255–76. https://doi.org/10.1177%2F0891243298012003002.

Moore, H. (2020). This process is freedom: The Ms. Q&A with lesbian separatist and anti-Klan organizer Trella Laughlin. *Ms.*, 2 March. https://msmagazine.com/2020/03/02/this-process-is-freedom-the-ms-qa-with-lesbian-separatist-and-anti-klan-organizer-trella-laughlin/.

Morioka, M. (2013). A phenomenological study of 'herbivore men'. *The Review of Life Studies, 4*(1), 1–20.

Munro, E. (2013). Feminism: A fourth wave? *Political Insight, 4*(2), 22–5. https://doi.org/10.1111%2F2041-9066.12021.

Musolff, A. (2014). Metaphorical parasites and 'parasitic' metaphors: Semantic exchanges between political and scientific vocabularies. *Journal of Language and Politics, 13*(2), 218–33. https://doi.org/10.1075/JLP.13.2.02MUS.

Newman, S. (2022). *The men*. Granta Books.

OED (Oxford English Dictionary). (2022). *'Manifesto' (noun)*. Retrieved 17 March 2023, from www-oed-com.ezproxy.lancs.ac.uk/view/Entry/113499?rskey=Xezn8G&result=1&isAdvanced=false.

Owen, T. (30 January 2020). US Coast Guard officer facing gun charges researched 'how to rid the U.S. of Jews', court docs reveal. *Vice*. Retrieved 4 August 2022, from www.vice.com/en_us/article/939kmv/us-coast-guard-officer-facing-gun-charges-researched-how-to-rid-us-of-the-jews-court-docs-reveal.

Panizo-Lledot, A., Torregrosa, J., Bello-Orgaz, G., Thorburn, J., & Camacho, D. (2019). Describing alt-right communities and their discourse on Twitter during the 2018 US mid-term elections. In H. Cherifi, S. Gaito, J. F. Mendes, E. Moro & L. M. Rocha (eds.), *Complex networks and their applications* VIII (pp. 427–39). Springer. https://link.springer.com/content/pdf/10.1007%2F978-3-030-36683-4_35.pdf.

Papacharissi, Z. (2014). *Affective publics: Sentiment, technology, and politics*. Oxford University Press.

Papacharissi, Z. (2016). Affective publics and structures of storytelling: Sentiment, events and mediality. *Informationl, Communication & Society*, *19*(3), 307–24. https://doi.org/10.1080/1369118X.2015.1109697.

Pavković, A., & Cabestan, J.-P. (2013). Secession and separatism from a comparative perspective: An introduction. In J.-P. Cabestan & A. Pavković (eds.), *Secessionism and separatism in Europe and Asia: To have a state of one's own* (pp. 1–19). Routledge.

Pearce, K. C. (2009). The radical feminist manifesto as generic appropriation: Gender, genre, and second wave resistance. *Southern Journal of Communication*, *64*(4), 307–15. https://doi.org/10.1080/10417949909373145.

Pearce, M. (2014). Key function words in a corpus of UK election manifestos. *Linguistik Online*, *65*(3), 23–44. https://doi.org/10.13092/LO.65.1402.

Pearce, R., Erikainen, S., & Vincent, B. (2020). TERF wars: An introduction. *The Sociological Review*, *68*(4), 677–98. https://doi.org/10.1177/0038026120934713.

Pedroja, C. (8 August 2021). Reddit bans 'Men Going Their Own Way' forums for violating hate speech rules. *Newsweek*. Retrieved 5 August 2022, from www.newsweek.com/reddit-bans-men-going-their-own-way-forums-violating-hate-speech-rules-1616379.

Preston, K., Halpin, M., & Maguire, F. (2021). The black pill: New technology and the male supremacy of involuntarily celibate men. *Men and Masculinities*, *24*(5), 823–41. https://doi.org/10.1177%2F1097184X211017954.

Radicalesbians. (1970). *The woman identified woman*. Retrieved 5 August 2022, from https://repository.duke.edu/dc/wlmpc/wlmms01011.

Reddit. (2020). *Promoting hate based on identity and vulnerability*. Retrieved 17 March 2023, from www.reddithelp.com/en/categories/rules-reporting/account-and-community-restrictions/promoting-hate-based-identity-or.

Reddit. (2021). *Reddit privacy policy*. Retrieved 17 March 2023, from www.redditinc.com/policies/privacy-policy.

Reisigl, M. (2014). Argumentation analysis and the discourse-historical approach: a methodological framework. In C. Hart & P. Cap (eds.), *Contemporary critical discourse studies* (pp. 67–96). Bloomsbury.

Reisigl, M., & Wodak, R. (2001). *Discourse and discrimination: Rhetorics of racism and antisemitism*. Routledge.

Reisigl, M., & Wodak, R. (2016). The discourse-historical approach (DHA). In M. Meyer & R. Wodak (eds.), *Methods of critical discourse studies* (3rd ed., pp. 23–61). SAGE.

Reskin, B. (1993). Sex segregation in the workplace. *Annual Review of Sociology*, *19*, 241–70. https://doi.org/10.1146/annurev.so.19.080193.001325.

Ribeiro, M., Blackburn, J., Bradlyn, B. et al. (2020). *From pick-up artists to incels: A data-driven sketch of the manosphere*. Retrieved 5 August 2022, from www .researchgate.net/publication/338737324_From_Pick-Up_Artists_to_Incels_A_ Data-Driven_Sketch_of_the_Manosphere.

Russ, J. (1972). When it changed. In H. Ellison (ed.), *Again, dangerous visions*. Doubleday. Retrieved 10 March 2023, from www.future-lives.com/wp-con tent/uploads/2014/09/When-It-Changed.pdf.

Savage, R. (2019). Evolve or die: The stark choice facing America's 'women's lands'. *Thomson Reuters Foundation*, 15 October. www.reuters.com/article/ us-usa-lgbt-women-idUSKBN1WU18C.

Scarabicchi, C. (2020). Migration manifestos in the 2010s: Performing border dissent between social action and utopia. *Language and Intercultural Communication*, *20*(2), 141–52.

Schmitz, R. M., & Kazyak, E. (2016). Masculinities in cyberspace: An analysis of portrayals of manhood in men's rights activist websites. *Social Sciences*, *5*(2), 1–16.

Shugar, D. R. (1995). *Separatism and women's community*. University of Nebraska Press.

Siapera, E. (2019). Online misogyny as witch hunt: Primitive accumulation in the age of techno-capitalism. In D. Ging, E. Siapera, E. & C. Soraya (eds.), *Gender hate online: Understanding the new anti-feminism* (pp. 21–44). Palgrave Macmillan.

Snow, D. A., Soule, S. A., & Kriesi, H. (2004). *The Blackwell companion to social movements*. Blackwell. https://doi.org/10.1002/9780470999103.

Sobieraj, S. (2018). Bitch, slut, skank, cunt: Patterned resistance to women's visibility in digital publics. *Information, Communication & Society*, *21*(11), 1700–14. https://doi.org/10.1080/1369118X.2017.1348535.

Solanas, V. (1967). SCUM manifesto. Reproduced in B. Fahs (ed.), *Burn it down! Feminist manifestos for the revolution* (pp. 217–45). Verso.

Star, S. L. (1982). Interview with Audre Lorde. In R. R. Linden, D. R. Pagano, D. E. H. Russell & S. L. Star (eds.), *Against sadomasochism: A radical feminist analysis* (pp. 66–71). Frog in the Well.

Stein, A. (1997). *Sex and sensibility: Stories of a lesbian generation*. University of California Press.

Sternisko, A., Cichocka, A., & Van Bavel, J. J. (2020). The dark side of social movements: Social identity, non-conformity, and the lure of conspiracy theories. *Current Opinion in Psychology, 35*, 1–6. https://doi.org/10.31234/osf.io%2Fwvqes.

Szenes, E. (2021). Neo-Nazi environmentalism: The linguistic construction of ecofascism in a Nordic Resistance Movement manifesto. *Journal for Deradicalization, 27*(1), 146–92.

Tarrow, S. (2011). *Power in movement: Social movements and contentious politics* (3rd ed.). Cambridge University Press. https://doi.org/10.1017/CBO9780511813245.

Taub, G., & Hamo, M. (2011). Dialectic textual negotiation: Redemption and sovereignty in manifestos of the Israeli religious settlers' movement. *Journal of Language and Politics, 10*(3), 416–35.

Trebilcot, J. (1986). In partial response to those who worry that separatism may be a political cop-out: An expanded definition of activism. *Off our backs, May, 13*. Reprinted in Gossip, 3, 82–4.

Troutman, D. (2022). Sassy Sasha? The intersectionality of (im)politeness and sociolinguistics. *Journal of Politeness Research, 18*(1), 121–49. https://doi.org/10.1515/pr-2019-0005.

Unter, P., & Kelly, N. (2020). The Heart (January): Lesbian separatism is inevitable. Retrieved 17 March 2023 from www.theheartradio.org/solos/2020/1/15/lesbian-separatism-is-inevitable.

van Dijk, T. A. (1998). *Ideology: A multidisciplinary approach*. SAGE.

van Dijk, T. A. (2023). Social movement discourse: Manifestos. In C.-R. Caldas Coulthard & M. Coulthard (eds.), *Text and practices revisited: Essential readings in critical discourse analysis* (2nd ed.). (pp. 113–33). Routledge.

Van Valkenburgh, S. P. (2021). Digesting the red pill: Masculinity and neo-liberalism in the manosphere. *Men and Masculinities, 24*(1), 84–103. https://doi.org/10.1177%2F1097184X18816118.

Vivenzi, L. (8 June 2018). Infiltrating the manosphere: An exploration of male-oriented virtual communities from the inside. *Diggit*. Retrieved 5 August 2022, from www.diggitmagazine.com/articles/infiltrating-manosphere-exploration-male-oriented-virtual-communities-inside.

Wachowski, L., & Wachowski, L. (1999). *The Matrix*. [Film]. Warner Bros. Pictures.

Wolf, D. G. (1979). *The lesbian community*. University of California Press.

Wright, J. H. (2004). *Origin stories in political thought: Discourses on gender, power, and citizenship*. University of Toronto Press.

Wright, S., Trott, V., & Jones, C. (2020). 'The pussy ain't worth it, bro': Assessing the discourse and structure of MGTOW, *Information, Communication & Society, 23*(6), 908–25. https://doi.org/10.1080/1369118X.2020.1751867.

Yan Eureka Ho, S., & Crosthwaite, P. (2018). Exploring stance in the manifestos of 3 candidates for the Hong Kong Chief Executive election 2017: Combining CDA and corpus-like insights. *Discourse & Society, 29*(6), 629–54. https://doi.org/10.1177/0957926518802934.

Young, H. (13 January 2021). Why the far-right and white supremacists have embraced the middle ages and their symbols. *The Conversation*. Retrieved 5 August 2022, from https://theconversation.com/why-the-far-right-and-white-supremacists-have-embraced-the-middle-ages-and-their-symbols-152968.

Zuckerberg, D. (2018). *Not all dead white men: Misogyny and classics in the digital age*. Harvard University Press.

Cambridge Elements ≡

Language, Gender and Sexuality

Helen Sauntson
York St John University

Helen Sauntson is Professor of English Language and Linguistics at York St John University, UK. Her research areas are language in education and language, gender and sexuality. She is co-editor of *The Palgrave Studies in Language, Gender and Sexuality* book series, and she sits on the editorial boards of the journals *Gender and Language* and the *Journal of Language and Sexuality*. Within her institution, Helen is Director of the Centre for Language and Social Justice Research.

Holly R. Cashman
University of New Hampshire

Holly R. Cashman is Professor of Spanish at University of New Hampshire (USA), core faculty in Women's and Gender Studies, and coordinator of Queer Studies. She is past president of the International Gender and Language Association (IGALA) and of the executive board of the Association of Language Departments (ALD) of the Modern Languages Association. Her research interests include queer(ing) multilingualism and language, gender, and sexuality.

About the Series

Cambridge Elements in Language, Gender and Sexuality highlights the role of language in understanding issues, identities and relationships in relation to multiple genders and sexualities. The series provides a comprehensive home for key topics in the field which readers can consult for up-to-date coverage and the latest developments.

Cambridge Elements ≡

Language, Gender and Sexuality

Elements in the Series

The Language of Gender-Based Separatism: A Comparative Analysis
Veronika Koller, Alexandra Krendel and Jessica Aiston

A full series listing is available at: www.cambridge.org/ELGS

Printed in the United States
by Baker & Taylor Publisher Services